PEEKABOO

OTHER BOOKS BY JEFF LENBURG

Steve Martin: The Unauthorized Biography
The Encyclopedia of Animated Cartoon Series
The Three Stooges Scrapbook
The Great Movie Cartoon Directors
Dustin Hoffman: Hollywood's Anti-Hero
Dudley Moore: An Informal Biography

*To Veronica Lake
and Constance "Veronica" Marinos,
with love*

Table of Contents

Preface

Peekaboo: The Story of Veronica Lake is a true, factual account of this former glamour queen's life, fully authorized by Miss Lake's mother, Constance Marinos, who was interviewed exclusively for the book. It was recreated as closely as was humanly possible; no scenes were fabricated for the sake of the story.

Each scene has been reconstructed from actual recollections told in interviews by friends, co-workers, members of the family, and Veronica herself.

Acknowledgments

The author is very grateful to the following friends, co-workers, and associates who provided insight and perspective while compiling this difficult biography: Eddie Bracken, Jeanne Cagney, Teet Carle, Joan Caulfield, Douglas Dick, Ann Doran, John Engstead, Bonita Granville-Wrather, Julie Gibson-Barton, Jan Grippo, Tom Hatten, Jack Hirshberg, John Houseman, Richard Lamparski, Richard Lane, Eddie LeRoy, Beverly Linet, Joel McCrea, Gary Owens, David Ragan, Matthew Rapf, Maurice and Louise Rapf, Mary Treen, Richard Webb, Richard Widmark, and Allan J. Wilson.

Also, I would like to take this opportunity to thank the following libraries and staffs for their untiring assistance: Thomas J. Watson of CBS Archives; E.S. Sampson of NBC Program Analysis; The Academy Arts and Science Margaret Herrick Library; California State University, Fullerton;

the *Los Angeles Times* Library; and the Anaheim Public Library.

Special accolades are owed to Dave Koenig for supplying the author with a complete listing of all *Photoplay* articles published on Miss Lake, and to Mike Lefebvre for his invaluable research. Also, a tip of the hat to Carol Cullen, Chris Costello, and Jordan Young for providing me with some essential data.

Greg Lenburg, whom I affectionately call "the master," also deserves credit for his comprehensive filmography and for suggesting the idea for this book.

I would also like to thank Greg and Cindy Gardner for loaning me their typewriter when necessary, and Pat Callahan for offering me a place to stay while conducting interviews in the Hollywood area.

Last, but certainly not least, my very special thanks and love to Constance Marinos for authorizing the work, and to Veronica's cousin, Helene Nielsen, for her support and guidance. And, of course, a special mention to my editor Ashton Applewhite, who has never failed to believe in me.

PEEKABOO

1
. . .

Years of Unrest

*T*HE YEAR WAS 1971; it was Veronica Lake's last hurrah. She had just returned to Hollywood from London after twenty years of exile, minus the customary fanfare or ceremonious frenzy that usually accompanied such momentous events.

Veronica was in town to promote her autobiography, *Veronica,* which had been drawing rave reviews from critics for its candidness. What Hollywood hadn't forgotten, though, were her years of unrest, her paranoid schizophrenic behavior, the unpublicized child beatings, the death of her infant son, scores of legal suits, her four disastrous marriages, and a studio system that had become weary of her rebellious nature.

During the last day of her promotional tour, Veronica was given a farewell party at the home of Rona Barrett, the famous critic and columnist. Barrett invited scores of old-time stars to what at first seemed more like a homecoming party than a going away bash. Mae West showed up to pay homage to this former star. Lucille Ball and her husband also made brief appearances, as did George Cukor, Howard W. Koch, Frank McCarthy, James Aubrey, Edith Head, the William Doziers, and even Pamela Cathcart (one of Veronica's stand-ins).

Veronica was no longer the delicate creature who had stirred a nation of male filmgoers to sexual fantasies. Her teeth were mostly rotted out and separated, her ertswhile peekaboo bang was nonexistent, her face was bloated from drinking and her cobalt-blue eyes were enveloped in thick bags of skin. She looked more like a boxer than a movie queen.

But to her friends and fans she was still Veronica Lake. Photographers scuttled around her for better angles, while streams of partygoers clustered like honeybees around this once-great star. From time to time small groups would splinter off to be replaced by larger numbers of attentive friends. Autograph seekers waited patiently outside Barrett's home, hoping to catch at least one glimpse of their screen favorite.

Veronica smiled for the photographers and acted very cordial during the entire affair, then, consented to one last interview with a local newspaper reporter. The reporter asked how she could have been so candid. Her reply was, "They say the book's frank. Well, that's a little off mark. If I had written everything I know about this town, there'd be a rash of divorces and at least a hundred people would die of apoplexy."

Veronica was so right. There was more to her life than first meets the eye. Her book made interesting reading but left many questions unsolved. Why did the studio cover up her unsuccessful attempt to miscarry her second baby?

Why was it that nobody (except possibly her mother) had paid much attention to her Jekyll-Hyde personality? Why had she become so cozy with Rita Beery, a self-professed lesbian and former wife of the actor Wallace Beery? These and other questions have never been properly answered.

Like many of her female contemporaries, Veronica clawed her way to the top, despite a series of handicaps, unprepared for the rigors of a motion picture career and not fully understanding her own potential.

The high point of Veronica's tumultuous career came during World War II. Her greatest moments on screen were in such classics as *Sullivan's Travels* (1941), *So Proudly We Hail* (1942), and her films with Alan Ladd, which included among others, *This Gun for Hire* (1941). In fact, Ladd and Lake went on to become one of the most popular romantic screen teams, ranking with Bogart and Bacall and Astaire and Rogers. Yet, through it all, her clashes with studio officials and her troubled private life marred what future she had on the screen.

She was born Constance Ockleman on November 14, 1922 (not 1919, as reported elsewhere). Her father was Harry Ockleman, a seaman by trade, who worked for the Sun Oil Company. Harry had met Veronica's mother, the former Constance Charlotte Trimble, in Brooklyn and it was there that Connie was conceived. Harry was of Dutch-German ancestry, and his wife was of Irish extraction. Connie was their only child.

The Ocklemans lived in a small, modestly decorated brownstone on Lifferts Avenue; Connie saw very little of Manhattan. Her only recollection was of the dirty snowfalls that cluttered the streets and lined the rooftops of nearby apartment buildings in the winter time. As she once recalled, "I didn't like my first snow. I was always a warm weather girl."

When Connie turned six she entered a local pre-school program and received her first taste of a formal education. The Ocklemans were a typical middle-class family. Harry worked steadily at a good-paying job that helped them meet their financial obligations. But his job required him to travel often, thus making it difficult for him to spend time with his wife and child. Therefore, it's safe to say Connie hardly knew her father. Two years later, the Ocklemans relocated, this time to Saranac, New York, where Harry had been transferred. Connie continued her education at nearby St. Angelo's Elementary School. Because Connie had been baptized and raised in the Roman Catholic faith, her mother insisted upon having her daughter educated in a parochial school. Her mother also preferred the Catholic school because class instruction would be on a more personal level than at the larger public school.

Connie was the toughest girl in the neighborhood. Boys had always enjoyed picking on her because of her tiny physique (she was to be only five feet one inch tall). But eventually she became fearless when she was called on to defend herself, and pretty soon, Connie became known in the neighborhood for her effective left hook. In an interview, she remembered, "I was the toughest broad on the block. I could whip 'em all. I preferred the companionship of little boys because girls would backstab and gossip all the time. Boys didn't."

Connie also preferred going barefoot, and wearing jeans and a shirt. Her cousin Helene Nielsen recalls: "Veronica hated getting dressed up. It was her mother who liked to dress her in frilly dresses, since she was old-fashioned and believed it was proper for all girls to dress up. But Veronica preferred to be just Plain-Jane. She wanted to be more relaxed."

Even without the aid of frilly or lavish dresses, Connie was definitely cute for her age. She had ocean-blue eyes, short blond hair, and soft, creamy skin. Her eyebrows were long and thin, and her legs were already nicely sculptured. Connie appeared to be a very attractive but still perfectly ordinary child: bright, lively, and not overly ambitious.

Unlike the other girls of her own age, she liked to play with fire engines and boxing gloves. Her favorite toy, however, was a set of paper dolls called "Baby Nancy." She would invite her next-door neighbor, Rosemary, to join her daily, and soon they became fast friends.

Eventually, Connie outgrew her toys and started to give them away to the younger children in the neighborhood. Harry Ockleman kept buying her new toys, to the delight of the neighborhood children. Her rascally contempt for trouble had already begun. When Harry finally caught on she was scolded royally—but it wasn't to be the last time.

Sometimes Connie's punishment included being separated from her friends. Connie was already known as the neighborhood loner, and her rebelliousness surely didn't help her to strike up many new friendships. "I didn't mind being alone sometimes, because I found solitude in that separation from people," she said.

In a short time, though, her attitude toward starting and maintaining new friendships began to turn negative. Connie's mother remembers that her daughter grew to expect all relationships to be unpleasant, thus causing her to become more aloof and detached from people. As Constance Keane-Marinos, Connie's mother, relates today: "I never thought she was having any trouble that most children don't naturally experience. I passed it off as nothing more than growing pains because her behavior seemed only natural." She also recalls another habit of her daughter's: "I could always tell who her last playmate was because she would mimic them to a tee while they played. I think she did it unconciously, but I was never sure."

Constance and Harry remained under the impression that their daughter's erratic behavior was merely an attempt to attract attention.

At the age of eight, Connie made her acting debut in the lead role of the St. Angelo's school play, *Poor Little Rich Girl.* (She had been handed the part because she had the longest, blondest hair in class.) In the show, she sang two songs and was dressed in a white bunny suit, winning both critical kudos from the audience and unanimous approval from both her parents, who had attended the premiere performance. Yet, despite her knack for it, Connie was no more committed to acting than to any of her other hobbies and interests. Her mother recalls: "She liked doing these school productions because she was usually given big parts. Then, one day, it was another thing, followed by something else the next day. You could never keep that girl interested in one thing."

Constance has described her daughter's childhood as being "a relatively happy one," but it came to an end in February 1932, when she was twelve. Harry Ockleman had been preparing his ship for launching off a Philadelphia dry dock, when a sudden gas leak caused the ship to explode. The explosion ripped through the ship's hull, killing Ockleman and his crew members instantly. It was one of the worst ship disasters in Philadelphia's history, and a personal tragedy for Connie and her mother. Although he had not been able to spend much time with his family, Connie's father had, from all reports, loved his wife and daughter. Financially, his death could not have been more ill-timed. Harry had just received his Master's papers, which would have entitled him to earn more money, money that he had planned to earmark for Connie's future.

Remembering the accident and how Harry's death affected Connie, Constance says, "She didn't know her father too well because he was away for months at a time. She didn't shed tears or anything. Instead, friends said, 'What a cruel kid she is,' because all she wanted me to do was buy her a bicycle. That's all she was worried about. Her behavior was really bizarre. I remember once when we met Harry at a dock in Miami, I said, 'Go kiss your daddy.' She said, 'You kiss him.' There was really nothing there."

Connie never asked why her father had had to be taken away so soon, a more normal reaction. According to her mother, Connie didn't really understand her own emotions. Constance did not understand Connie's reaction and continued to grieve over the loss of her husband. But she also knew the importance of her daughter having a father. A year later she married one of her closest friends, Anthony Keane, a staff artist with the *New York Herald*. Keane had known Constance for years and was one of the Ocklemans' frequent visitors.

Not a rugged man like Harry, Keane was gentle and kind, though firm when he had to be. He loved to hold Connie. His gentleness made her instantly comfortable, and for a time, brought them closer together. From the start there were questions about Connie's relationship with her stepfather. She has said, "I liked my stepfather, although I didn't know him very well and he in no way served to replace my father." She adopted a new name, though: Constance Keane.

As she grew older, however, Connie began to resent her stepfather. According to her mother, Harry's frequent long absences and then his death made Connie dislike the idea of having a father figure around the house. The dynamic in the young girl's head may have been: Just when you think you can count on a person for a little support, they fail you. Afterward, she adopted the irrational viewpoint that her life was destined to be filled with constant catastrophe, with Harry's death as only the beginning. What wasn't known then, however, was that this is a characteristic commonly linked with schizophrenia. As Constance Keane-Marinos explains: "I think she started hating Anthony, because she had this built-up hatred toward her real father that she carried over when I married Anthony."

Connie's life took another unhappy turn when she was enrolled in another private school, this time the Villa Maria Convent School in Montreal, Canada. It was an all-girls Catholic boarding school, with an annual tuition of nearly two thousand dollars. Two local Saranac priests had persuaded her mother to enroll Connie in the school. Connie revolted against going to Montreal and being separated from her parents, but Constance assured her young daughter that it was the best thing to do. With Connie gone, home was quieter for Anthony, who had contracted tuberculosis and was undergoing treatment. Even so, Keane continued drawing for the *New York Herald* while Constance held down her job with the local hospital to help pay for Connie's schooling.

But Connie hated her new surroundings. All the girls were required to wear regulation clothing—a dull black dress with a high collar—and Connie rejected such regimentation. She became the school's number-one troublemaker, and a frequent visitor to the office of Mother Superior, the school's principal.

Day after day enraged nuns would drag Connie out of the classroom. She often fought with other students. She stuck gum under desk tops or in students' hair, and, in general, used her imagination destructively. When confronted with these accusations, she denied them emphatically. But when face-to-face with Mother Superior, it was a different story altogether. Mother Superior would greet her every time with an expressionless face, as if prepared to strike down the child for her misdeeds. Once Connie's escorts left them alone, however, Mother Superior would become surprisingly jolly, breaking into a wide grin and asking, shaking her head, "Constance, Constance. What am I going to do with you?"

"I don't know," Connie would impishly reply.

"Do you know all the trouble you've caused?" Mother Superior would ask. "It's been enough for an army."

As if compelled to make trouble the order of her day, Connie would reply, "I know. But I can't help it."

"Well, you have got to stop, Connie," Mother Superior would order politely. "That's, of course, if you plan on staying at this school."

Not another word had to be uttered. Then, following the silence, Mother Superior would ask Connie to promise her one last thing: "Would you please control your rebellious nature, Connie? Do that for me and yourself. Now promise me."

Fully aware that she wouldn't keep her word, Connie's reply was always the same: "I promise, Mother Superior. I promise."

In spite of Connie's promises—and Mother Superior's rapport with the defiant young girl—Connie was simply too disruptive for the closed community to handle. The school released her in the summer of 1937. Constance tried to sympathize, but she was disappointed over Connie's head-strong ways. Rather than take her to a psychiatrist for a thorough examination, Constance felt that a change of scenery would do her daughter good. Thus, in the fall of 1937, the Keanes went to Florida for four months, and enrolled their fifteen-year-old daughter in Miami High, where beach parties, jai alai, and football were the major preoccupations. It soon became apparent that Connie preferred the citrus groves and warm sunshine of Miami to the cold, damp wintery months of Montreal.

Connie had not yet dated anyone, largely because she would withdraw whenever she was around her fellow classmates, as well as people in general. There was no other explanation for her behavior at that time, other than that she was "shy." It was much deeper than that, however. As it was diagnosed later, she was rapidly developing into a paranoid schizophrenic, completely terrified of everyone around her and convinced that others were talking or plotting against her. It is hard to determine why she developed such a personality, and the whole situation baffled Constance and Anthony.

It was when Connie began attending Miami High, though, that Constance noticed her inability to make new friends. When she was younger she had alternated between being friendly with other children and preferring her own company. But now, as her mother recalls in an interview, "Connie was very nonsociable and always clung to herself. As weeks went by, I finally asked her, 'Haven't you gotten acquainted with anybody yet?' She'd say, 'No, I haven't. And I don't want to . . . I don't want to.' It was only later that she became a belle of the ball because a country club near the school held dances every Friday night and she would go. She had seventeen formal dresses when she was only fifteen."

Connie's sudden outgoingness wasn't abnormal for her condition. Doctors have found that schizophrenics occasionally break out of their shells to try to make new friends. Some have extended periods of normal behavior. They return to their closed-in personalities only when they become hurt, or feel threatened. That was exactly what happened in Connie's case.

It took place when she experienced her first crush. The boy in question was the school's quarterback, Frankie

Rentz, the high school heartthrob. Connie often had passionate daydreams about Frankie, though her sexual fantasies never exceeded the usual necking, for she was still rather naïve about sex.

Her crush lasted until Connie landed a Christmas job wrapping packages at the Blue Cross Drug and Department Store on Flaglen Street in uptown Miami. Connie was doing very well on her new job until the day Frankie walked in and began searching along the cosmetics counter. Connie just had to talk to him. She stepped down from her wrapping post to help Frankie, hoping that he might ask her out.

"I didn't know you worked here," Frankie said, pleased to see her.

It was the first time she had ever spoken to him, but she mustered up a weak, "What can I do for you, Frankie?"

"Oh, I'm looking for some perfume."

"For your mother, I suppose?"

"Oh, no. I'm buying it for my steady girlfriend."

Connie's heart sank. She tried not to show that her feelings had been hurt, but inside her temper had begun to boil. Connie was not only a rebel at heart, but extremely vengeful whenever the situation called for it. To get even, she selected the most expensive and worst smelling bottle of perfume in the store!

Afterward, she did date several other boys from the school. None of them caught her fancy like Frankie Rentz had, though, and it is perhaps here that she began to believe in her inability to sustain any long-lasting relationships, to believe that she was unable to be loved and that she was incapable of loving. Many young teenagers have these feelings, but with experience learn that they can relate to people. Connie probably never was convinced that she could love or be loved.

It was on her fifteenth birthday that Constance became

convinced that her daughter was suffering from some type of mental disease. She knew something was seriously wrong. Connie had always been difficult and her behavior had seesawed erratically between withdrawal and spectacular outbursts. To these, she now added periodic delusions. "She always had these delusions and believed in them. I remember when we had guests over for her fifteenth birthday, she told everyone that on her first birthday party she had sat in a high chair and that I had baked a cake with one candle on top. I am a gourmet cook, but a baker I am not. In fact, I never baked a cake in my entire life. She dreamed the whole thing up."

Mrs. Keane took Connie to see a psychiatrist, but Connie resisted. She was very defiant toward doctors and nurses, fearing that they were all out to harm her. Even though the psychiatrist diagnosed the illness as paranoid schizophrenia, Constance was unable to convince her daughter to continue with the psychiatric treatments. "The problem was she would never follow through with her appointments," Constance says. "She would never show up. Instead, she'd go once or twice, then say, 'I can outsmart them.' And she did. I felt so helpless, never knowing what I could do next."

Connie was crafty all right. After several more tries with various other psychiatrists, Anthony finally convinced Constance to give up trying. He flatly stated, "Take the fifty bucks [the psychiatrist's fee] and buy yourself a new hat."

2

. . .

Hollywood or Bust

CONSTANCE KEANE JUST DIDN'T SETTLE for less whenever her daughter's future was concerned. Connie's health was of paramount importance to her, as was her career. She wanted her to take advantage of her natural beauty by eliciting it for public gain. But Connie might not have been mentally and emotionally prepared for such endurances.

Show business offered everything that Constance wanted for her daughter: a full-time career, money, and glamour. But Connie wasn't certain whether she wanted a career in Hollywood's film factory. Still convinced her daughter's future was in film, Constance saw to it that Connie was steered in the right direction. Usually, Connie didn't question her mother's good intentions, but as the years passed Connie's rebellious nature would surface repeatedly.

And by now, Connie's high-school days were also numbered. The school principal would call Mrs. Keane daily to report a new disciplinary problem. "She was very disruptive in class," her mother recalls. "Not that she did anything mischievious, it was just that the boys in her class couldn't keep their hands off her. She was very beautiful for her age. She was fifteen but looked like she was twenty-one. But when problems at school persisted, we had to have her removed." Connie hadn't changed much from her days at Villa Maria.

Meanwhile, Connie had decided to join a sorority. The initiation ceremony included just one catch: each sorority applicant had to enter a Miami beauty contest. Lacking the essential confidence and frightened over what people would say about her, Connie nevertheless persisted because the club would offer her a chance to make new friends.

Around this same time, a local Florida publicist named Steve Hannagan began organizing several Miss Miami beauty contests in the area. Contestants were individually photographed at hotel poolsides or on Miami beaches, and their pictures were published in newspapers serving cities such as New York, Baltimore, and Cleveland to drum up business and interest.

Connie heard of Hannagan's contests and, despite her severe feelings of inadequacy, entered one to meet the sorority's membership qualifications. Out of one hundred participants, she became the eighty-sixth and tried on several occasions to back down out of the competition at the last minute. But her prospective sorority sisters were determined to see her go through with the contest, even if it meant dragging her up on stage.

To prepare for her performance, Connie experimented with her entrance in front of a mirror at home.

Staring at her reflection, she straightened her shoulders, swiveled her hips, and practiced stripping off her long, black satin dress to reveal her tightly fitting bathing suit. Connie would at least impress the judges with her ability to wiggle her rump.

The night of the pageant, the band struck up some introductory music as master of ceremonies Harry Richman announced, "And ladies and gentlemen, here we have contestant number eighty-six, Constance Keane." Connie strutted out on stage with her shoulders pulled back, trying to cover up her nervousness. She knew the judges would scrutinize her every move and vote on her gracefulness as much as her abundant beauty. At just the right moment Connie unzipped her dress, flung it to the floor, whirled around with the enthusiasm of a cheerleader, and raced off stage to thunderous applause.

Backstage, emotions ranged from depression to hysterics to enthusiasm to anxiety. Nobody knew what to expect—not even Connie. She joked with several other contestants, saying that she didn't have a fighting chance at winning.

To her complete surprise, Richman walked up to the microphone and announced, "And our third-place winner, Constance Keane." Connie covered her mouth in her hands and jumped up and down in excitement, both shocked and overjoyed at her triumph.

Afterward, Richman went backstage to congratulate her. Constance wasted little time in taking some of the credit for her daughter's victory. As Richman shook hands with Connie, she interrupted. "Mr. Richman, I'm Connie's mother, Mrs. Constance Keane."

"It's a pleasure to meet you . . . you have a fine daughter here," Richman enthused.

Mrs. Keane nodded happily. "Yes, I think so."

"In fact," Richman thought aloud, "she has the clear makings of a star. She'd make it in Hollywood for sure."

Connie stood frozen over Richman's words, while her mother savored the master of ceremonies' enthusiastic remarks. Mrs. Keane beamed proudly, wrapping her arms around Connie, saying, "You're certainly right, Mr. Richman. She does have what it takes." Persistent as usual, she tried to see if Richman would back his comments with a commitment to help her daughter make it in show business.

"Mr. Richman, so you say my daughter would make it in Hollywood?" Constance asked, hoping to turn her dreams of Connie's stardom into a reality.

Pausing to choose his words carefully, Richman said, "Your daughter showed real showmanship tonight, Mrs. Keane. And I think she would make it if she had the *right* people behind her."

Connie was awestruck. She was not used to such words of encouragement. Not even her mother had ever lavished her with such adulation. Connie didn't understand that her mother's critical remarks, both negative and constructive, were intended to help build strong character. Instead, Connie would bridle over her mother's remarks, although she never voiced her displeasure until much later.

While Connie won membership into her school's sorority, her participation in the club lasted less than a week. Her interests continued to shift restlessly and, according to Constance Keane, Connie's attention span could never be held to one specific interest for very long. "That is why she never had a formal education. She refused to study or carry out class assignments. She rebelled [against] the very nature of the school's curriculum. So when she left high school altogether, I didn't know what else to do but help her with her future."

It didn't take much persuasion on Mrs. Keane's part to

guide her bewildered daughter down the right path. Connie's mother next entered her in the Miss Florida contest, the largest in the state. The contest appeared tougher at the outset, as her opponents were even more stunning than her earlier competitors. But Connie surprised everyone—including herself—when she took first-place honors. Her picture appeared in all the local newspapers and helped establish her identity in the community. The victory was short-lived, though, as judges disqualified her immediately afterward: Connie was only fifteen; participants had to be at least eighteen.

Connie took the news in stride, and then some more good news came her way. The director of recreation from the Flamingo Hotel in Miami Beach saw her stage presentation in the beauty contest, and was interested in having her as a permanent employee. Telephoning Mrs. Keane, the director told her, "You have a very beautiful daughter. Would she be interested in working for me?"

It turned out that the hotel needed a talented swimmer to work in an aquatic act with one of Hollywood's zaniest comedy teams, the Ritz Brothers. Constance accepted the offer on her daughter's behalf, informing the gentleman that she could start the next day. Whether Connie herself was anxious to perform, her mother cannot recall, saying only that "Connie was a very good swimmer, because she took swimming lessons as a child, so she was a natural. The job was hers for the taking, but, like everything else, she lost interest quickly. I couldn't understand why. At first, I thought it was just part of growing up."

Although Connie's watery antics were brief, they did attract attention. A scout named Bill Grady, who was on assignment from Metro-Goldwyn-Mayer, caught one of the shows and introduced himself to Connie's mother afterward. He said, "If you're thinking of having her go into pictures, let me have first claim on her." Mrs. Keane was agreeable so long as the terms were right. Satisfied, Grady wired MGM to inform Irving Thalberg's secretary, Mertle Tuttle, of the potential contractee he had found. Metro's initial reply was, "We're not interested at the present time."

Disappointed, Constance and Anthony decided to abandon the tropical state and return to their home in Saranac, New York. After resettling, Connie heard from MGM a second time. This time around they wanted to make a screen test to determine whether they should put her under contract.

On June 27, 1938, the Keanes set off on their cross-country trip in a Chrysler Airflow, along with Connie's cousin, Helene Nielsen, who also had similar show business aspirations. Connie was eighteen when she first saw Hollywood. According to Nielsen, Connie had no burning desire to make the screen test, but did so to please her mother. "Connie wasn't the type to get up and be exploited. She was very withdrawn, but she did what she was told. She listened and followed her mother's instructions until she outgrew them. Then, her rebellious attitude really came out, because she had been building it up inside for quite some time."

Surely, Connie had every right to be apprehensive about what Hollywood had in store for her. She had heard all the gossip about this legendary land, with its romances and palatial mansions. She envisioned a dashing leading man sweeping her off her feet and taking her away to some uncharted tropical island.

That was Connie all right, always the dreamer, mixing fantasy with reality. Such delusions of grandeur were only intensified as her exposure to Hollywood's dream factory increased. She would tell her parents' friends that she used to live in a twenty-three room mansion, or that her father was a millionaire several times over, or that her family tree was linked to royalty.

Outsiders never questioned these delusions since Connie always gave a resounding performance, and her stories seemed quite harmless at first. Aware that these exaggerations were symptoms of illness, Constance later regretted not following her instincts. But she felt helpless since Anthony didn't believe they could help Connie.

Connie went to Saturday afternoon matinees at local theaters as often as possible. Her favorite films were action-adventures and comedies, in some of which, she was able to watch the likes of such popular femme fatales as Jean Harlow and Mae West, never realizing that some day she'd join them on the silver screen.

Connie saw her first real movie star at Dolores', a local restaurant, where she ordered hamburgers and Cokes for the family. Ann Shirley, a popular film ingenue at that time, was the actress in question, and of course Connie reacted like any star-struck youngster. Connie stared at Shirley in disbelief, pointing her out to her mother. Constance was known to capitalize on such situations, but this time, she showed a little more restraint than she usually did. She urged Connie to sidle over and introduce herself. But Connie stood dead in her tracks, staring until Shirley finished her hamburger, paid the hostess, and drove off.

Afterward, Connie was simply delirious. She had seen her first movie star and was more excited every minute over the prospects of living in Hollywood. She wanted to head back east immediately, in fact, to tell everyone just who she had seen. But the Keanes made their move permanent when they rented a small apartment on Oakhurst Drive in Hollywood.

Connie had gone along with Anthony to pick it out

while Constance went shopping, and as Constance Keane-Marinos remembers, Connie and Anthony became quite close to each other at this time. "Connie did everything with him. She'd tag along no matter where he was going. Sometimes, in fact, people thought he was her wife. When they went looking for apartments, one manager said to my husband, 'You have a very lovely wife.' He said, 'She's not my wife, she's my daughter.' It always surprised everyone when they found out how young she actually was."

Comfortable in her new surroundings, Connie spent most of her time with her cousin, Helene. The two girls attracted their share of attention. Although Connie was very petite, she was very well-built for her age—and she knew it. She enjoyed taking advantage of her beauty in a teasing manner, but only for the sake of fun as Helene Nielsen recalls: "Connie didn't have to flirt with the boys at all; they flirted with her. I'd walk down the street with her and they'd all whistle like wolves in the night. I was too afraid and wasn't into the boys then. Neither was she."

From time to time Connie started having serious thoughts about becoming an actress. But her first several months in Hollywood were a complete waste of time. MGM cancelled the screen test indefinitely, leaving Connie stranded. Trying to keep her occupied, Constance enrolled her daughter in the Bliss Hayden School of Acting on Wilshire Boulevard. Connie started classes in September 1938 and quickly became friends with some other girls in her class who had been working as extras in films.

While she found her studies at Bliss Hayden "sometimes less than stimulating," Connie acted in various plays. Her instructors' harsh criticisms only made her try harder the next time around. Connie performed exercises for her posture, balancing unwieldy books on her head and walking to the beat of a metronome. She likewise practiced her acting skills at home under her mother's tutelage. Constance had big plans for her daughter; she knew Connie had something special going for her, and wasn't about to stop now.

But Connie's indifference stood in the way. Constance says, "Connie made friends quickly there but she was so indifferent to everything. I remember her instructor called me up one night and said, 'I don't think Connie's going to go on tonight, she doesn't know her lines.' She ditched school to have lunch or something. She just wasn't interested in any particular thing, and I guess that would include acting."

Soon, a local talent agent began dating Connie and tried helping her toward her mother's career goals. As Connie once remembered:

> Mother suggested [that I go out with] a certain man about town, whom I had met shortly after my arrival and who seemed to know everybody. He had asked to take me out several times previously but I had always refused. Still, he was so persistent that I finally went with him. But I didn't have a very good time. He was kind of fat and too bluff and breezy; the kind of man who always calls you "Baby" and just can't keep his hands off you. There was always an excuse for an arm around you, or a plump hand on your elbow. Somehow I didn't feel quite comfortable with him.

Connie, instead, credits one of her school friends, Gwen Horn, for helping her land her first professional acting job. Gwen had heard that Paramount Pictures was casting extras for its film, *All Women Have Secrets,* starring Jeanne Cagney and Peter Lind Hayes. Released to theaters in the spring of 1939, the film dealt with a college girl's romance and ultimate marriage to a university science professor.

Initially, Connie didn't want to attend the auditions as she was afraid she'd fail, but Gwen convinced her to try first. Both reported to Paramount, anxious to prove their hidden acting abilities. They soon learned that they didn't have to act much. Extras were chosen on the basis of whether they looked like the type of people casting directors wanted; it was that simple.

Connie was elated at the news that she had been selected, along with Gwen, as one of a dozen extras. Connie's mother was probably the happiest of the trio. She told her daughter this was the start of a promising career, but that she would have to work constantly if she wanted to succeed.

Connie's screen debut required only one day of work, for which she earned sixty-five dollars. In her only scene in the film, Jeanne Cagney (Jimmy's sister) announces her engagement to a college professor as a swarm of sorority girls, including Connie, congratulate her.

Cagney recalls Connie's brief appearance: "I was known around the set as 'Chatty Kathy,' because I usually talked to everyone. Connie was a darling little girl with golden blond hair. She didn't have it in the peekaboo cut yet. I was in only one scene with her, and, afterward, we all became like family. It was hard to part when it was all over."

Connie began showing her first signs of self-assurance when she tried for her second minor role in *Sorority House*. The film starred none other than Ann Shirley and was released in 1939. Her friend Gwen Horn also went along to RKO Studios for an audition. Sorority girls must have been in vogue then, as they landed similar roles in this film as well. For her performance, Connie wore a dress that Ginger Rogers had worn in an earlier RKO musical. In fact, she liked the dress so much that after the picture was over the director let her keep it.

Connie socialized as much as she could on the set and was more at ease this second time around. She even found time to converse with Ann Shirley, but was hesitant to confess that they had met unofficially at a local restaurant. The reality of working in films hadn't even set in.

Connie's next bit part was in an RKO three-reeler with Leon Errol entitled *The Wrong Room* (1939), in which she played a child bride. (By this time, Connie had acquired the services of Barney Ross, an agent who worked for a small agency in Hollywood. Ross handled all of Connie's business affairs until she signed with Paramount, at which time Constance shifted her to the William Morris Agency.)

Next, Connie moved to Metro-Goldwyn-Mayer, home of Leo the Lion and movie mogul Louis B. Mayer. It was the same studio that was originally supposed to have her film a screen test, but that all seemed inconsequential now. MGM signed her for her fourth role in the Eddie Cantor feature, *Forty Little Mothers,* released on April 26, 1940.

Before production started, Constance noticed that her daughter was coming home later and later each evening, using the age-old excuse that she was "out with friends." It turned out that Connie was spending her leisure time at Ciro's, matching her drinking ability with other patrons at the restaurant. Nobody seemed to know she was under age —she was only seventeen—and her drinking went on unnoticed by her parents for almost three months. But that soon changed when Connie's mother found out. Apparently, the pressures of Hollywood had already gotten under her daughter's skin, but, more importantly, doctors had warned Constance that alcohol would only advance Connie's schizophrenic illness.

As Constance once said:

First, I started taking her to another psychiatrist for help. But she kept missing appointments and after a short time of therapy, the doctor said to me, "Leave her alone, there's thousands of them walking around the streets who all belong in institutions." After that, she kept returning to Ciro's. She was an alcoholic at seventeen. So, instead of doing nothing, I contacted the attorney who handled Charlie Chaplin's paternity case. I informed him of her condition and the drinking problem, and he wanted to have two men pick her up at Ciro's and afterward put her through a psychiatric hearing to determine whether she should be put away. I thought it over but couldn't go through with it. I should have done something, but her career stood in the way of right and wrong. I didn't want to be accused of ruining her career, or becoming known as one of these hateful mothers.

Teet Carle, an MGM press agent at the time, first met her on the MGM lot. He reported no traces of any hangovers from her late night binges, and fondly recalls that "Connie was very enthusiastic, wistful, and very sociable. She was always bubbling up to everybody in the publicity department, and was eager about publicity. In fact, all of us called her 'Little Connie.' She'd always come over and find somebody to talk to, maybe some newspaper reporter, about horseracing, or anything, even if she didn't know anything about it. She'd pull it off. But when the picture was finished, she went on her merry way."

Several people agree that Connie's drinking may have temporarily released her from her withdrawn state, causing her to be unusually outgoing. It's also possible, because of her feelings of insecurity, that she was reaching out to others for moral support.

During production of *Forty Little Mothers*, Connie decided to try out a new hairstyle. Up until this point, she had worn her hair in ringlets. But for this performance, she came up with the idea of wearing her hair down for the first time. She had long, blond tresses that were shoulder length and naturally curly, without the aid of a curling iron. Her bob of hair had a tendency to lose its bounce and would sometimes drop over her right eye. During one scene, Connie's hair did exactly that.

Known around the studio for his occasional temper tantrums, Eddie Cantor became enraged. He stalked the set like a madman. "What the hell was that? Did you see that!" he growled. "Her hair just ruined the scene."

The director, Busby Berkley, whose MGM musicals kept filmgoers spellbound by their brilliance, disagreed. He quickly countered Cantor by saying, "Eddie, a little hair isn't going to hurt one scene. I like it. It brings a certain charm to our little girl."

Cantor growled even louder. "She and her hair have destroyed this scene. They go, or I do."

Berkley stood firm, saying, "I'm keeping her and her hair in whether you like it or not . . . that's final!" And thanks to Berkley, Connie could be identified easily because her coiffure distinguished her from the thirty-nine other girls in the scene.

3
...

The Case of
the Accidental Hairdo

*T*HE RELEASE OF *Forty Little Mothers* failed to produce an avalanche of movie offers. Putting her hair back behind her ears, Connie felt she was doomed to a life of obscurity.

During her nonworking hours, Connie spent a lot of time strolling through the MGM backlot, watching stunt men take risks in some big-budget western or the filming of an important romantic scene in an *Andy Hardy* film, and rubbing elbows with some of the studio's most celebrated superstars. Connie's afternoon sojourns down Metro's magical backlot only enhanced what vivid dreams she had left about becoming a star.

Connie was treated as royally as any member of the MGM movie family, receiving the same benefits and privileges as the studio's full-fledged stars. She often lunched at the commissary among Metro's producers and directors, in hopes that maybe she'd be discovered.

Connie's dreams of stardom drew closer, however, when, one day, she met Metro's new talent director, Freddie Wilcox. Wilcox, formerly a Miami newspaper reporter, had become good friends with her stepfather. Spotting Connie on the MGM backlot, he shouted after her to wait. He said, "Connie, don't you remember me? I'm Freddie Wilcox. I know your father." He didn't look familiar to Connie. Nevertheless, Wilcox continued, "You know, I'm a pretty good director. Have you ever seen any of my films?"

Connie wasn't sure what to say, but felt compelled to answer. "Oh, yes. I've seen your films, Mr. Wilcox," she stated flatly, without emotion. "They're good."

Flattered, Wilcox asked her to drop the "mister stuff." He then queried, "What do you do around here?"

Choking back her nervousness, Connie remarked, "I've been working in films as an extra. I was supposed to make a screen test here, but that never happened." As it dawned on her that maybe Wilcox could help her, she broke out of her customary indifference, rambling off the list of titles, their casts and characters, and the running times of each of her film performances with the speed and exuberance of a used-car salesman.

She continued her spiel, but Wilcox now appeared less interested in her credentials. There was *something* that attracted him to her, but exactly what it was, he wasn't sure. Eventually, he concluded that it was her hair. He said, "Connie, how about making that screen test? Let me help." She agreed, and Wilcox said he would set up a filming date. She probably wanted it for herself, but Connie also knew it would be the only way to keep peace with her mother.

Connie's biggest mistake was telling her mother about the test. Constance relished the thought that her daughter was taking a step toward stardom. She overreacted and, according to Connie, started telling her what to do, how to act with Wilcox, until Connie finally ran out of the room, confused and crying. She wanted to tell her mother to butt out of her life, but because she herself was so insecure and because she did have some respect for her mother, she left well enough alone.

That week Connie reluctantly called Wilcox to arrange for the test and became extremely nervous afterward. With each new day, her tension mounted, her stomach wound up in knots, and she grew more restless. She'd brush her teeth constantly, or read a book (never past the first page), or talk with her girlfriends over the phone, trying endlessly to expel her nervous energies. As the film date drew closer, Connie tried convincing herself that maybe she wasn't cut out to be an actress. But although, as always, she felt inadequate, she didn't really believe that. She also started wondering if other actresses had suffered similar mental anguish. As she explained in an interview: "I thought the price of what I was after was too high, and decided to forget the whole thing. I did, then success sought me out, and Hollywood came to me."

It actually didn't happen quite that way, but that was as close as Connie could remember. With the pressures becoming too great, she spent most of her evenings at Ciro's, drowning her fears in one glass of vodka after another. She managed to escape her mother's surveillance by saying she was going to the studio.

The morning of the test, Connie's mother smeared her daughter's face with makeup, and critically assessed her posture, outfit, and expression. The whole idea annoyed Connie, who complained that she hated getting dressed up. But Constance had her way. For the test, Connie wore a slinky, white chiffon dress, her hair tucked behind her ears.

As the camera began rolling, she tried to give her best performance, but kept fumbling over her lines. She couldn't remember them. Freddie Wilcox, who was directing the scene, tried making the footage a technical master-piece, putting the lighting men, prop men, and sound tech-nicians through their paces. But the one element that didn't function was Connie.

Wilcox shot take after take, hoping that Connie would fall into some type of groove. She didn't. After finishing the test, Wilcox whispered to the cameraman, "It's no use. She doesn't have it today."

Problem was, Connie knew it too. She returned home, and without making a report to her mother, closed her bedroom door and sobbed helplessly. What had she gotten herself into?

Then, in March 1940, Connie's luck changed drasti-cally. While out on casting calls, flowers were mysteriously delivered to the Keanes' home one afternoon, sent to Con-nie from a secret admirer. Constance grew suspicious. "What's this?" she barked, shoving the flowers in Connie's face the instant she arrived home.

Connie couldn't answer. She didn't know.

"Are you seeing someone? 'Fess up if you are."

Connie was equally curious to find out who had sent them. It certainly wasn't a gift from an old boyfriend, since she hadn't had many dates after arriving in Hollywood. In the days ahead, Constance continued to wonder as the delivery of flowers continued. Every Thursday, for one full month, Connie received a new bouquet of flowers from her nameless admirer.

Then, one day, the admirer finally broke his silence and called Connie. He was John Detlie, an art director at Metro. Like Freddie Wilcox, he had noticed her walking briskly along the studio backlot. He obtained her address from the casting department and sent flowers until he had worked up enough nerve to phone her.

Wasting little time, John asked Connie and her mother to lunch the next week at the Brown Derby. Constance was impressed by Detlie's professional decorum, his maturity, and the fact that he had established his own career. At the age of thirty-three, he was sixteen years Connie's senior, but that didn't seem to matter. Constance was hopeful that his usefulness could be twofold: that he would date Connie and help advance her career.

The following Tuesday arrived and so did John, this time to take Connie shopping. "She'll be out in a minute, unless she's completely crazy," Mrs. Keane told him as she opened the door. "Right now, she's spying on you through the crack in the door down the hall. She wouldn't trust my judgment."

After that, Connie and John went out unescorted practically every night. They rode the merry-go-round at Ocean Park, consumed big candy apples, and drove home over hills soft in the starlight. Constance noticed that there was a new warmth in her daughter, in her voice, and in her eyes, the result of John's constant attention.

Constance worked out one snag in the relationship early, however. She imposed a 1:00 A.M. curfew on Connie's dates with John. Connie broke curfew only once: on her first date alone with John at Ocean Park. She missed the deadline by two hours and for punishment she was kept home every night the following week. It was Constance's way of laying down the law, hard and long, and illustrated her protectiveness of her daughter.

Connie's mother operated by the old school. The man in question had to be polite, neatly dressed, considerate, and had to ask her first for the opportunity to date her daughter. Prior to John, there had been one other man who fit that bill, Jack Jordan. As Constance once recalled:

Connie was worldly-wise because I instructed her on everything. I know that men would tell me after they took her out, "You don't have to worry about her, nobody could touch her with a ten-foot pole." She was a good person when she had to be, especially when she went out with this Jack Jordan. He was the heir to some candy manufacturer and was left with a ten thousand dollar-a-month income. He took Connie out quite frequently, before she was a star. He also had a ruby necklace he inherited, which he kept in a safe-deposit box. One night, when he asked Connie to dinner at Sir Cedric Hardwicke's, he asked my permission beforehand on whether she could wear this jewel. I said yes, but my husband didn't approve. I said there was no reason why not since he really didn't have to ask, he was just being honest. He could have waited until they got to the car to put it on her. So, she went out with some very nice people, until she got into pictures.

Constance also had emphasized proper manners and table etiquette during Connie's upbringing. Curtsying in front of guests was mandatory until her fourteenth birthday, at which time she asked her mother, "Mother, do I have to curtsy anymore?"

While her relationship with John was going strong, at Paramount her name was circulating through the rumor mill. Producer Arthur Hornblow, Jr. was casting his wartime blockbuster, *I Wanted Wings,* which paid homage to our nation's top aviators lost in battle during World War II and starred Ray Milland, William Holden, Wayne Morris, and Constance Moore. With his main cast set, Hornblow kept searching for exactly the right girl to play an unsympathetic siren—a nightclub singer named Sally Vaughn.

Fate stepped in, in the guise of Hornblow's secretary, Veronica Grusling. It seems that Hornblow had received a copy of Connie's original screen test produced by Freddie Wilcox, but had refused to see it. Hornblow's secretary interceded and used persuasion to change the producer's mind. He viewed the test all right, but thought it stunk. However, something about Connie hit a responsive note and he requisitioned a second test.

It was Saturday morning and Connie was washing her hair for a date with John when the phone rang. She answered it with a towel wrapped high about her head.

Grusling said, "Miss Keane, this is Arthur Hornblow's secretary at Paramount calling. How tall are you, please?"

"Five feet one inch," Connie answered suspiciously.

"Thank you," replied Grusling. "Good-bye."

That was all she heard from Grusling for several days. Before the next unsuspecting call, disaster struck again. John and she double-dated with Constance and Anthony at a restaurant off the coast in Santa Monica. Anthony was still suffering badly from tuberculosis, but had been able to function normally. Suddenly during dinner, he started to complain about a pain in his chest, followed by a shortness in breath. His left lung had collapsed. Constance recalls:

During dinner, he said he wasn't feeling good. So John said he would drive us home. We immediately hopped in the car and managed to get home. Then, I called some local doctor and said, "Do you know anything about tuberculosis, because I've been in California for only about a year, but my husband's suffering very badly." He said, "Frankly, no, for the past three months I've been in an internship." He came over anyway and did what he could. Then, we had a 'round-the-clock nurse there to help. When he had the collapsed lung, though, his heart shifted over to the other side and afterwards he developed a heart condition, which plagued him the rest of his life.

As doctors and nurses tended to him at home, Constance became so hysterical from watching her husband gasp for air that she had to be sedated. Connie remained rather calm throughout the entire ordeal. Inevitably, thoughts of her father's death ran through her mind. Would this mean another death? All night Connie worked with the nurses. Her father's bed had to be changed again and again. Trying to revive his weakened lung, nurses gave him glucose and morphine injections, but Anthony was too weak to even bend his arm.

In the meantime, Connie tried giving her mother some strength and some of her courage, saying, "Daddy's going to be all right. You must believe that, you just must. . . ." By five o'clock in the morning, her father had finally fallen asleep. Then, one of the nurses told Connie, "You lie down too. I'll call you when he wakes."

The nurse woke Connie at seven, and three hours later Veronica Grusling from Paramount called. She said, "You're due here for a wardrobe fitting, right now! We want to make another screen test."

Connie quickly washed and dried her hair, called John to tell him what was happening, and dashed off to the studio. This time around she knew that all the marbles were at stake. If she failed, she'd struggle helplessly as a bit player the rest of her life.

When Connie reached the studio, she was ushered through makeup. Then, her hair was set. Next, wardrobe assistants pinned and basted her into a dress covered with bugle beads, telling her, "You'll look all right as long as you don't turn around."

In the scene, Connie played an alcoholic nightclub siren, drunk and slumped over the club's bar. Ted Weaks directed the test. (He also served as director of *I Wanted Wings*, until he was replaced—for reasons that will be discussed later.) Weaks had arranged for William Holden and Richard Webb to appear in the test with Connie. Wiping her nervousness away, Connie thought of her stepfather's ailing condition and how she wished she could be at home to comfort him. In fact, a dozen or more times during filming she said, "If you won't need me for a few minutes, I'd like to make a call. . . ."

The test's start was also temporarily postponed when Connie received a large package, handsomely wrapped in cellophane, and delivered by messenger. Inside the bright wrapping was a toy panda. Connie adored pandas. A note hung from the stuffed animal's ear. It read: "Good luck. With all my love, John." Connie hoped that the panda symbolized good luck and began filming while the panda sat on the sidelines in the director's chair.

Even though the test began late, Connie soon learned that the director was "a bust man." Richard Webb, who knew Connie from the Bliss Hayden School of Acting, remembers that test. He had left the school to take on a job at the Warner Brothers Theatre on Hollywood Boulevard. In an interview, Webb recalled the circumstances that followed, as well as the screen test:

I had an interview at Paramount in March of 1940. I did a reading and received big accolades and was hired as the senior cadet in *I Wanted Wings*. On April 6, 1940, the studio called and said, "We want you for a test we're going to do with some girl." Bill Holden showed up, and the director, Ted Weaks, followed. Connie came dressed in a little sailor hat and sailor suit and Weaks said, "Oh, God, get her out of here. Go dress her." So they took her over to wardrobe and brought her back to the set in a metallic dress, and she was very well endowed. This director was the type who cut the legs off his chair, so his butt was about an inch off the floor. And he always talked in a low voice, so you had to go over and bend down to hear him. Connie did— and boom! Her breasts fell right out. Well, the director was a bust man, because afterward he moved me out and Bill out of the camera range, with us just voices coming over the test. The camera was focusing tightly on Connie's body, nothing else. The peekaboo hairdo came at the same time during the test, when her hair suddenly began hanging down.

Webb insists that the mismanagement of her hair bothered Connie because she "wasn't used to it. She usually wore her hair back when she was off screen." The director was also another major concern since, according to Webb, he wanted to take her to bed. As he tells it: "I don't know how far he got. He was trying to get closeted with her, but I don't imagine he ever succeeded. I'm sure she resisted, knowing Connie."

John Engstead, an art supervisor at Paramount, also recalls that Weaks was taken with Connie. As Engstead says: "I first heard of [Connie] from a director named Ted Weaks. He stopped me on the lot, mentally drooling. 'You should see the girl I have to play in the film. She's got bosoms out to here,' he said, cupping his hands in front of him. 'In fact, yesterday, while making the test, an electrician up on the catwalk just about fell down leaning over to see down her dress.' "

Since Connie was all business, it's hard to imagine Weaks succeeding. The only nuisance was her hair. During the test, Connie tried shaking her hair out of her eye, only to become more and more exasperated, and finally leaving in tears when the filming was completed. Afterward, Connie was ready to take a pair of gardening shears and cut her hair down to size. Convinced that her hairdo had ruined the test, she returned home and sulked for days. Her mother was anxious to learn the results. But Connie lied and said, "I did great, Mom. Just great." Then she burst into a torrent of tears and slammed the bedroom door behind her. In fact, she even missed the screening of her test to producers. As she once recalled: "I felt I blew the test. I had my arm on a table, it slipped, and my hair—which was babyfine and had this natural break—fell over my face. It became my trademark, and purely by accident."

Connie also cried for another reason. She was hurt by what she heard after the test was finished. A cameraman walked up to her and said, "Good test. The first thing you saw was this big nipple, followed by five minutes of body." Covering up her real reaction, Connie laughed loudly with the cameraman, But, when she got back home, her true emotions surfaced. She was upset that Weaks chose to exploit her physical features instead of her acting abilities. She felt she had failed yet again.

Several days later Hornblow phoned and asked her to meet him in his office. At the meeting, Hornblow appeared weary, sleepless, a crumpled man, as if the weight of his project had become a heavy burden. The burden was Connie. The reaction of the studio heads to her test was less than overwhelming. But Hornblow had cast the deciding vote, convincing Paramount's brass that Connie was right for the part. Connie was keenly aware that her acting needed improvement, though she was surprised to learn that Hornblow liked one element the most: her hairdo. "You've got the job," he said. "But leave your hair alone."

Hornblow was sold on the magnetism Connie evoked on the screen, the kind that made superstars. But he did suggest that she make one change. "Connie Keane is a cute name," he said, "but filmgoers associate in their mind the person with the name. And you just don't look like a Connie Keane." Hornblow admitted that he had slept very little the night before because he was trying to concoct a new screen name for her. As he explained, "Your eyes have the coolness of a lake, and you look more like a Veronica, which is my secretary's name. So let's call you Veronica Lake."

Connie nodded in agreement. She just loved the name —and Veronica was also the name most people called her mother. But Connie's biggest thrill was that Hornblow had chosen her over the other girls tested. With her new name and hair in place, Connie started production of *I Wanted Wings* on August 23, 1940.

She left Hollywood for the shooting location in Texas, but was unhappy at the thought of leaving her boyfriend, John, with whom she had fallen deeply in love. John continued to show his adoration for her, sending her flowers pinned to a second panda. (This was the beginning of a vast collection of pandas, numbering almost a hundred, all of which would be accompanied by deliveries of flowers from John.) Connie started having thoughts of running away with John, of marrying him and settling down. But for her, the future had just begun.

4
···

Peekaboo

LITTLE DID VERONICA REALIZE that what she considered her greatest nuisance—her wavy, naturally languorous hair—would some day become her greatest asset. In *I Wanted Wings,* she would officially unveil her "new look" hairdo and launch herself as America's newest sex symbol, one filmgoers would affectionately call "the girl with the peekaboo haircut." It also marked the first time she would receive billing under her new name: Veronica Lake.

Starring in her first major motion picture definitely overwhelmed Veronica. She knew the first rule of movie-making was survival of the fittest, so she did everything possible to protect herself from getting trampled upon. Veronica sensed that some of her co-workers would have enjoyed watching her fall flat, but she rose to the challenge. Paranoid that others were plotting against her, she withdrew psychologically, and never displayed on the set the typical astonishment associated with neophyte actresses. Instead, she came across as tough, cocky, and aloof from the people around her.

On location in Texas, Veronica bounded on to the set each morning with the vivacity of a newborn kitten, ready to claw her way to the top. She was often the first to arrive and rehearsed her lines alone, never asking anyone for help. Veronica made one or two half-hearted attempts to strike up a camaraderie with her co-workers, but it was no use. Kibitzing wasn't her specialty. It only made her feel uneasy since she knew some of these very same people felt threatened by her youthful presence.

According to most of her co-workers, Veronica was a perpetual loner on the set, an image she upheld through-out her career. Richard Webb says, "I don't remember her with any particular group of people. Just herself. She didn't pal around with anyone, but then again, that just didn't seem to be her nature. She also didn't discuss her private life, nor did she she seek any kind of help. Sometimes we would meet and have lunch together, but that was the ex-tent of her relationships on the set."

There were several other occasions when the realities of filmmaking—its pressures and anxieties—broke into Veronica's private world, causing her to reach out for help. Veronica has said that although she wasn't popular she got along with everyone except Constance Moore, the film's female lead. She shared living quarters with Moore when the filming shifted to San Antonio, Texas. Each had their own private bedroom with connecting bath and living rooms. But Moore was known among her contemporaries as the last of the Texas Swingers, a social butterfly who partied nightly until four or five the next morning.

Veronica didn't attend these social gatherings because

she took her work very seriously, retiring early to bed to refresh herself for the next day's filming. In the meantime, Moore held her all-night bashes on the floor above, keeping Veronica up all hours of the night. But Veronica never complained. In search of a remedy, she quietly visited the company doctor, who prescribed sleeping pills. But the blaring music, popping of champagne corks, and the clinking of glasses overcame the pills' effects.

As Veronica was afraid of Moore, she voiced her complaint to the assistant director. The assistant said he could move her quarters to the sixth floor. Veronica moved upstairs, and it took Moore approximately a week to notice. When she did, however, all hell broke loose. She never let up on Veronica, constantly harassing her, calling her names, and informing others what "a baby" she was.

Such derogatory remarks deeply hurt Veronica, who was still sensitive to people's comments about her. She was only nineteen and in the early stages of a promising movie career, but she was an immature, emotionally unstable girl.

When Moore's badgering finally cracked Veronica's composure, she phoned the film's producer, Arthur Hornblow, who was at Paramount Studios in Hollywood. Near tears, Veronica pleaded, "I don't want this, Mr. Hornblow. Can't you find somebody else? Can't you!"

Hornblow remained rigidly calm, giving her fatherly guidance. He told her, "Don't worry, Veronica. I'm in your corner. I'll see that it stops."

It did. One phone call to director Ted Weaks, and Moore was given a muzzle for her trouble, which in time proved to be only temporary.

It was at this point that Veronica started thinking about John. She missed him and his endless supply of compassion, often fantasizing that he would suddenly appear on the set and take her away. She had already had enough. Veronica preferred dreaming about settling down in a private, secluded cottage far away to the reality of the Hollywood grind. But she was only pretending to herself. She had second thoughts about her career, and decided to stick it out to see just how far it would take her. She didn't like the pressure, but she did like her prospects.

During filming of *I Wanted Wings,* several mishaps occurred. Ray Milland and Brian Donlevy, the two stars, were naturals in their roles as wartime pilots. Milland and Donlevy were both former pilots and actually flew their own aircraft during many of the film's scenes. The film's flight adviser, Lieutenant Gray, would tag along to make sure that everything went smoothly. But he didn't sit inside the cockpit, the natural position for a co-pilot. Instead, hidden from the camera's view, Gray would lie on the wing opposite the plane's fuselage and hang on as either Ray or Brian took the craft airborne.

One time, while coming in for a landing, the throttle accidentally jammed and caused the plane to keep gaining speed, spinning out of control, and flipping Gray off the wing. His head just missed the plane's stabilizer, and he sustained only minor injuries. Nobody else was hurt in the accident, but, according to Veronica, "It certainly didn't make me crazy about flying."

The film's director, Ted Weaks, made very few friends during the production of *I Wanted Wings,* including the official brass at Kelly Field, where most of the film was shot. (Kelly Field was an Army Air Corps base where pilots were training for the war.) Paramount eventually fired Weaks and replaced him with Mitch Leisen, a relative newcomer to directing. Richard Webb recalls what caused Weaks' dismissal:

Weaks was fired off the picture, and for good reason. While shooting out on the runway with scores of training pilots flying overhead, he turned around to a major general and screamed, "Get those planes out of here!" Now, bear in mind that that picture was government-sponsored. Well, it was Saturday morning when that happened, and Sunday evening here he came out of the hotel with his bags and baggage as Bill Holden and I were seated in the lobby. Veronica wasn't with us, she was up in her hotel room. On Sunday morning, Mitch Leisen came in with all of his bags and baggage to take over the picture.

There was apparently no love lost between Veronica and Weaks, because she admitted having constant trouble of "a personal nature" with him. As a matter of fact, she informed Paramount that "Either he goes or I go," which was quite a bombshell coming from a newcomer. Weaks had wanted to seduce her since the screen test and kept up his pursuit daily. Married or unmarried, she wasn't interested. When the cast learned that Paramount had fired him, Veronica couldn't have been happier. With the film grossly over budget, the studio was particularly displeased that Weaks had let his personal life interfere with the film's completion.

Mitch Leisen was quite a character in his own right. A former assistant to Cecil B. DeMille, he had accrued a sparkling list of credits including *The Volga Boatmen, King of Kings,* and an earlier aviation feature, *Thirteen Hours.* Leisen turned out be good friends with Constance Moore and her husband, film director Johnny Maschio. Moore informed Leisen to keep a watchful eye on Veronica since she was "a troublemaker." Veronica kept her hostilities to herself, staying on guard at all times.

But Leisen was more interested in the male actors on

I Wanted Wings. He pursued just about every man employed in the film, including Richard Webb, who recalls:

> Mitch Leisen was an exotic director. He worked best with females. Mitch was gay, and he made his pitch to me down in Texas. He'd have me up in his suite every night and the cast and crew were betting odds when I was going to be bedded by him. He finally made his last pitch: "You think I'm abnormal." Everything he said, I'd say the opposite. I said, "No, Mitch, I don't . . . I like women." He got up, went in his room, put on his dressing gown instead of a chemise he had on, and came back. From then on, we were good friends and he didn't make any more advances.

Veronica probably welcomed the change. Yet, even with a new director on the set, she never broke out of her cocoon to socialize. Webb invited her several times to join him and William Holden for a couple of drinks at the La Toppa Tia, a local nightclub, but she declined. Holden and Webb practically put the La Toppa Tia on the map, drinking together there after filming was over for the day. Although Constance considered Veronica an alcoholic, at this point in her life, Veronica kept her drinking as private as the rest of her personal life. No more friendly socializing like the early days at Ciro's. It's possible she sneaked down to the La Toppa Tia to drink by herself, but she never went with anyone from the set. Whenever she was on the road, she usually drank in the privacy of her own room, ordering beverages from the front desk. John was unaware of her drinking, something that he would only discover much later, after they were married.

Aside from alcohol, John was the only other comfort in Veronica's life. He was her prize panda. Every night, after wrapping up filming, she would phone John, and they would exchange endearments, and she would tell him her troubles. She definitely yearned for his love. By now, they each had their own nicknames. Veronica enjoyed calling John "Pops," because of his advanced age; John likewise enjoyed called her "Mousie," because she was, so to speak, as thin as a mouse. Veronica only weighed ninety-eight pounds. Like other couples in love, John and Veronica often talked about marriage, and Veronica promised that once filming moved back to California they would discuss the subject at greater length.

Before packing for Hollywood, however, Veronica spent her last day in San Antonio posing for a series of publicity photographs to help promote *I Wanted Wings*. She was a very photogenic and cooperative model, bending into whatever position the photographer requested. But, then it happened: one take went awry. She was standing within touching distance of a B-17 bomber. While the photographer kept snapping away, the pilot of the aircraft, unaware that Veronica was near, started the engine as she was leaning over in a fashionable and sexy pose. The prop wash caught her dress and gusts of wind blew it up around her thighs, creating quite a titillating sight for innocent bystanders. With a surprised look on her face, the photographer captured what would become Veronica's most famous pose.

It was included in all advance publicity mailings for *I Wanted Wings,* appearing in newspapers and magazines all over the nation. The response was deafening. Reporters from around the country kept calling the studio to arrange interviews. Filmgoers wanted more information on the new ingenue named Veronica Lake. But Veronica was too unsophisticated to fathom what was happening and why suddenly everybody wanted a piece of the action—in this case, more of her.

However, this was not half as embarrassing as another camera blooper—one that was censored before it went out to the public. The incident became known around the Paramount lot as "the photographers' boob-boo." The photographer in question was Gene Richie, who worked under Paramount's art supervisor in charge of all staff photographers, John Engstead.

In an interview, Engstead recalls how he handled this very delicate situation:

> Gene Richie and I did a sitting with Veronica. Richie was one of the studio's portrait men. Veronica photographed very well, poised, with her hair down over one eye. She never had many glamorous clothes, so I had to search with Edith Head's help through the women's wardrobe department for a glittering, sexy dress. We found one that had been made for Jean Arthur for *Easy Living,* made out of solid beads. Veronica was small, not tall, and the only thing big were her bosoms. Edith said the dress would stretch and that Veronica could get it over said bosoms. Veronica put it on and it did stretch. During the setting, Gene and I had her lying around and at one move, one of the large baubles fell out. The dress stretched too much. But, funny thing, Veronica didn't know it was out and went on giving sexy, one-eyed looks. When Gene and I were wondering how to tell a girl her bosom was hanging out, she noticed the lull in the proceedings, looked down, and covered her face in embarrassment, putting the unruly thing back in her dress.

Back in California, Veronica immediately resumed filming at the company's new location at the March Air Force Base in the tiny community of Riverside, which was about one hundred miles east of Hollywood. To her delight, John was waiting for her. He came to surprise her, providing even a bigger surprise once they were alone: he asked Veronica to marry him. She kissed him over and over, and accepted his offer with no ifs, ands, or buts.

Veronica and John filed their intention of marriage secretly on September 26, 1941. They planned to elope to a little chapel in Santa Ana, California, the following evening without saying a word to anyone about their plans. Not even Veronica's mother was to know.

As Veronica once remembered: "I always loathed the idea of a formal wedding and I was determined not to have one. I didn't want those who loved me weeping while I was married. I also didn't want others speculating about my gown and other things. When you're getting married, I think you want to think about getting married, not feel like you're on parade."

Veronica agreed to meet John in front of the designated chapel at nine o'clock where they would be married by a justice of the peace. She hoped this would become the turning point in her life: a permanent bonding that would provide much solace. She would have someone who loved her and wanted to protect her. She would now become a woman.

The following evening, John made his escape to Santa Ana, waiting for Veronica at the chapel. Meanwhile, on location, Veronica was growing tense. The dress she had hoped to wear hadn't come back from the cleaners, so she borrowed a flaming red dress the studio owned that had been worn by Betty Grable. She then softened the effect with long black gloves and a black bag.

Filming didn't end until eight o'clock, going overtime, and leaving her with only an hour to reach the chapel. Riverside was thirty-five miles east of Santa Ana and there were no freeways connecting the two towns. Veronica stopped at her hotel room to pick up some bare necessities, only to find her mother and father waiting for her. "Daddy's so much stronger today," her mother told her, "that we thought we'd come for dinner to surprise you."

Surprise her was an understatement. It's unlikely Veronica had ever pulled off a finer piece of acting than her efforts at eluding her parents. Unsuspecting, her father said, "Are you working very hard?"

"Hard—and long!" Veronica said dramatically, wiping the imaginary sweat from her brow. "Tomorrow, for instance, I have to be up at five o'clock and I have pages—simply *pages*—of dialogue to learn tonight!"

Her parents started gathering their wraps, saying, "You go directly to bed. We understand."

Waving them down the hotel steps, Veronica flew upstairs to grab her panda and her overnight case, before hailing a cab. She told the driver, "Make time. I'll pay for any tickets. And stop at the first drugstore we pass. I have to make a telephone call."

By the time the driver found a drugstore it was already a quarter to nine. She called the chapel rectory to advise the minister that she was on her way. But unfortunately, Veronica arrived forty-five minutes late—to find no John. Clutching her panda, she waited inside the chapel perched on the edge of one of the pews. Finally, the minister's wife came in, patted her shoulder, and said, "John will be back in a minute. He went to get something to eat." Minutes later, John returned, grinning, and holding a bouquet of baby gardenias for Veronica to carry up the aisle.

The wedding ceremony went on as planned, and John slipped a wedding ring that he had designed himself on Veronica's left hand. It was carved in the shape of a tiny panda with a diamond perched on a crest in the center.

Sealing the ceremony with a kiss, they jaunted off to their private honeymoon retreat, a posh Spanish-style hotel downtown.

Later that evening, in a complete daze, Veronica crawled into bed and wondered to herself what the future would hold. Cuddling up tightly to her husband, she said, "Tell me you love me, John. You do, don't you?"

Cradling her in his arms like a piece of expensive porcelain, he reassured her. "Yes, I love you, Veronica. I do." In the same breath, John added that he wanted to drop the nickname, "Mousie," in favor of one that he thought was more mature: "Ronni," which became her moniker from that night on.

As the sun's rays carressed the face of his slumbering wife the next morning, John grew suddenly concerned whether marrying someone as young as Veronica was a mistake. He also wondered privately whether stardom would change her, and whether he would ultimately stand in the shadows of her career. But he dismissed such notions immediately.

The marriage was the best-kept secret in town. Studio executives frowned upon their young stars marrying because it supposedly dampened their sex appeal if filmgoers knew they were attached. It also dismayed studios because marriage denied them the proper chance to publicize their starlets as glamour girls. Fortunately, Paramount wouldn't experience this same dilemma with Veronica . . . not yet anyway.

It was a sorry state of affairs, however, when Veronica's mother learned of the marriage. She was heartbroken to think that John, whom she trusted implicitly, would run off with her only daughter without even asking permission first. In an interview, Constance remembers her reaction to the news: "I was very much annoyed at her. In the first place, we were all devout Catholics and she never went to the studio without stopping in at the Good Sheperd on the way to say a prayer, believe it or not. John was also divorced, which I never knew. As it turned out, he was too soft for her anyway. She needed someone who would give her a good kick in the butt every so often."

John Detlie's stepfather, Jack Grant, formerly a chief motion picture reviewer for *Hollywood Reporter,* was just as furious. Grant revealed to Paramount press agent, Teet Carle, that, frankly, he found Veronica bizarre. According to Carle, Grant didn't feel his stepson's marriage was one of those made in heaven. "I can remember after they got married, I saw Jack Grant for the first time in months. He informed me about the wedding, and I said, 'Oh, yeah, well, she's a great girl.' He said, 'Yeah, well, there's no reason for ever marrying that gal.' I said, 'What are you talking about?' He said, 'There's something wrong with her, that's all.' I told him he was wrong, but he disagreed."

Veronica and John rented a small apartment outside Hollywood, accenting the living room in chintz, blue-gray, and yellow. They hung John's paintings on the walls, and built shelves in the bedroom for all the toy pandas John had given her. Her collection of pandas grew as John discovered other reasons to love her.

Veronica resumed filming the morning after the wedding as if nothing had happened. Even though her parents and the Detlies knew within a day or two, she kept the marriage under wraps at the studio. In the meantime, John departed for Gallup, New Mexico, to wrap up production of his own film. *I Wanted Wings* completed its own location filming and returned to Paramount to finalize all integral shots.

During the final phase of production, however, Mitch Leisen became antagonistic, suddenly treating Veronica mercilessly. Constance Moore was apparently the villain behind it all, telling Leisen that Veronica was bound to make trouble. In fact, when Veronica flubbed a dance sequence with Ray Milland, Leisen tore into her, his temper seething, calling her "the dumbest bitch I've ever seen."

Veronica broke down in tears. Ray Milland came over and sympathetically put his arm around Veronica to console her. He told her, "Never cry. Once they spot any flaw in the armor, they'll take advantage of you every time." Remembering this lesson, Veronica tried becoming stronger, more withdrawn, and more unreachable. Veronica became afraid to show her emotions, her anger, or her frustrations openly. She feared losing everything she had worked for—and also feared what she might do if someone uncorked her emotions.

But Leisen never gave up. He took every opportunity to belittle her. Whatever other reasons he had, it was too late to force her to quit with three-fourths of the film completed. Veronica knew this, but her barrier of resistance cracked once more following another one of Leisen's vicious remarks. This time she sobbed for an undetermined length of time inside her dressing room. Afterward, she carefully plotted her revenge. She would have the final say, swearing to herself that she would, even if it meant losing her job.

Veronica's emotions were tested again that same afternoon. She received her complimentary copy of *Hollywood Reporter* and was reading it during a break in filming. An item in one of the morning gossip columns allegedly reported that Veronica was having an affair with another actor. Exactly who she was linked with, or what the column said, isn't known. It is known that Veronica saw this item as an infringement of her privacy, but then she didn't realize that such gossip was commonplace in Hollywood. While most actresses would have thrown the paper aside, Veronica continued reading and pretended that this bit of gossip didn't bother her. But it did.

Meanwhile, shooting was about to resume. The assistant director shouted, "No one go away. We'll be rehearsing any minute. We're already behind schedule." Veronica paid no attention to this warning. She sat glumly in her chair on the set while some cast and crew members, obviously bored, tried passing the time by joking around with her. One technician cracked, "What is it they're going to call you for advertising purposes—The Blond Bombshell?"

Everybody laughed but Veronica, who managed a small smile. Seeing that Veronica was piqued, William Holden wisely stepped in before an eruption occurred. He told her, "Don't let them get you down, Miss Lake." It didn't help. Tears spilled from Veronica's catlike eyes. She pushed back her chair, ran to her dressing room, and returned later when filming resumed and her temper had cooled.

The next day, filming began on schedule, but Veronica was nowhere to be found. Leisen organized a search party of crew members to check the dressing room and studio commissary. But Veronica had vanished. Nobody remembered spotting her that morning, not even the studio guard. The commissary's hostess also had no recollections of Veronica strolling in for her usual cup of coffee. Leisen was dumbfounded.

That morning, Veronica had hopped in her 1939 Dodge and headed for Gallup, New Mexico, to join John. It was her way of telling Hollywood, its gossip columnists, its star system, and Mitch Leisen to "go to hell." It was also typical of her schizophrenic nature: she would often become a fugitive of her personal woes rather than deal with them openly.

By evening she pulled into Needles, California, staying

overnight and resuming her journey at dawn. She wanted to tell John how much she loved him and hear how much he loved her. All he had to say was the word and she would give up her career, gladly. Back at Paramount, Leisen continued with his frantic search for Veronica. The studio placed an all points bulletin out for her. Private investigators were hired to track down her whereabouts.

But Veronica's well-planned trip almost ended in tragedy. It was Thanksgiving Day, and it was snowing heavily. Every few miles, Veronica had to get out and clear the snow from the windshield in order to see. The course she had charted included winding mountaintop roads that were slippery when icy. Veronica lost control on a steep downgrade. Her automobile tumbled over the side of the road, crashing over rocks and through underbrush, miraculously rolling to a stop at the edge of the cliff. Nobody heard her cries for help. Shortly, the horror of the accident set in. She first noticed that her toes had been broken. Then, moving her left knee, she realized it had been torn as well on the car's steering column. She had also sustained tiny lacerations on portions of her face, and her dress was bloodsplattered.

Somehow, Veronica squirmed out of the crushed vehicle and crawled back up to the road. There she flagged down a ramshackle truck carrying a farmer, his wife, and a small son headed for the Ozarks. They stared in disbelief at Veronica's blood-smeared appearance. Looking suspiciously at her, the woman asked, "Where you aiming to go?"

"I'd like you to drop me off at Flagstaff," Veronica said weakly, her face pale. "I'll pay you. . ." Veronica collapsed in a puddle of blood.

The farmer immediately took her to the Flagstaff Automobile Club where a truck was dispatched to tow her car in for repairs. Meanwhile Veronica was driven to Gallup where she received medical care from a local doctor. The physician treating her said, "You have two broken toes and you've cut yourself badly. You haven't suffered too much —so far—because the cold icy snow acted as an anesthetic." The doctor quickly tended to her bruises, and tucked her injured toes into a small walking cast.

John was informed of his wife's accident by the automobile club and came as quickly as possible. He accompanied Veronica back to his hotel room, where they dined together for the first time in almost a week. It was then that the shock of the accident really set in. Crying, Veronica clung to John, whimpering that she was glad to be alive.

But John was flustered. He was naturally most concerned about his wife, but he knew how the studios operated. "Maybe you should call Paramount."

"They don't know where I am," Veronica admitted. "And I'm not sure I want them to know."

Veronica had told John earlier about the gossip column item, but he appeared unconcerned. He knew it was part of the Hollywood game. Holding Veronica safe in his arms, he said, "You should have never come here. If you're going to be a star—and I have a hunch you are—we'll both have to get used to columnists." Veronica wasn't so easily convinced, but she nodded lamely in agreement. She did not make the phone call.

It took Paramount almost three days to trace Veronica's disappearance to the small town of Gallup. The studio's private investigators had ferreted her trail to the mountainous cliff where her car went off the road. Thereafter, the secret of her marriage was out and the firm foundation for her career slowly began deteriorating.

Veronica received an irate phone call from a studio executive, chastising her for walking out. He warned that she'd never work in Hollywood again if she didn't return to work promptly. Thanks to the likes of Mitch Leisen and Constance Moore, Veronica had been characterized as a spoiled brat and was, thereafter, branded throughout Hollywood as "a constant troublemaker." As the executive told her, "You're holding up production. You've jeopardized an investment of hundreds of thousands of dollars because of a . . . a whim. We can't have people who do such things."

"I'm not the girl for you then," Veronica told him. "You'd better replace me with someone who doesn't care what happens to her private life as long as she gets ahead."

"Well, uh . . ."

Stopping the executive from interrupting, Veronica warned, "I didn't ask to work for you, remember. You sent for me. I'll hand in my notice right away."

Paramount heard the message loud and clear. Veronica's outburst over the phone changed the entire picture. It was agreed that Veronica would return to work when she was able and that, in the meantime, they would shoot around her, filming the scenes in which she didn't appear. Not bad for a newcomer.

In an interview, Veronica recalled her feelings and reasons for pulling the incident:

> It was my first contract and I knew from nothing. I was a young bride in love. You know that no girl in love ever thinks clearly about anything. John was the finest man I had ever known. Well, I know it was silly but I ran away because I got bawled out [by Leisen]. I thought my feelings had been trampled on that time, but a real blow taught me how gentle life had been on me till then. The blow hit before Thanksgiving Day when during a break in filming I read in a gossip column that I was supposedly fooling around with

another man. Today, it is easy to say I would have laughed. But then I couldn't take it that way.

But what else might one expect from a nineteen-year-old girl, a paranoid schizophrenic at that, engulfed in the troubles of the real world, a world which she'd rather escape from. As Veronica herself said: "I'd established myself in the hearts and minds of Paramount as a temperamental little brat with the arrogance of a nobody."

Veronica's indifference toward the studio also made news in syndicated columns nationwide. In his daily column, "Town Called Hollywood," Phillip Scheuer reported that "Miss Lake professes indifference to the stardom her sponsors are deliriously thrusting upon her, and is already being viewed with alarm as a problem child."

It took many months for the studio to patch their differences with Veronica, but, meanwhile, showing good faith (and having had her own way) Veronica returned to Hollywood to finish filming of *I Wanted Wings*.

By the time *I Wanted Wings* was released nationwide to first-run theaters, filmgoers were well-informed about Veronica's debut as a major film star. Paramount had lived up to its reputation of manufacturing stars by turning out mammoth amounts of publicity on Lake, including studio biographies, magazine articles, and scores of posed cheesecake photographs. One press release enthused: *"I Wanted Wings introduces in Veronica Lake a personality the studio believes to be another Jean Harlow or Clara Bow. She plays the part of a feminine 'heavy' in the film and dies in a plane crash in the final sequence. Producer Arthur Hornblow, who selected Veronica after her tests topped those of more than a score of ambitious new actresses, believes she has many of the qualities which made Bow and Harlow stars of the first magnitude."*

Drumming up much early exposure, *I Wanted Wings*

opened to critical acclaim at New York's Astor Theater on March 26, 1941. The film dealt, in flashback, with the fate of three Army Air Corps enrollees: Ray Milland, Wayne Morris, and William Holden. Brian Donlevy portrayed their tough Air Corps instructor, and Veronica appeared as a husky-voiced cabaret singer (her song, "Born to Love," was dubbed by Martha Mears, who sang for Veronica in all of her films).

Filmgoers and critics agreed that Veronica was both stunning to look at and had talent that should be watched. As Archer Winsten of the *New York Post* reported: "She displays more acting ability than one expects for one so young and sleek-looking, thus arousing anticipation of her future appearances." Besides her obvious acting prowess, Veronica's hairdo also won rave reviews as Howard Barnes of *The New York Times,* in tongue-in-cheek fashion, wrote: "She has a startling hairdo, with overlong tresses that she occasionally strings out as though she was about to use her head as a violin."

It was also her sex appeal and histrionic persuasion on the screen that caused Cecila Agers of *P.M.* to remark: "Miss Lake is supposed to be a femme fatale, and to that end it was arranged that her truly splendid bosom be unconfined and draped only ever so slightly in a manner to make the current crop of sweater girls, by comparison, a bunch of prigs."

Veronica on screen projected an aura of mystique that would be hard to match. But it was also her hairdo that would grab much attention in the months ahead and clearly establish Veronica as the decade's most recognizable sex symbol.

5
· · ·

The Hairdo
That Rocked the Nation

*W*ITH *I WANTED WINGS* a smash hit, Veronica's career skyrocketed. She became an instant household name due to the studio's enormous outpouring of publicity. Veronica knew her own market value was rising. Thus, her first issue with Paramount's executive board was her salary. She asked for an immediate salary hike, but not in the usual manner associated with such contract negotiations. Processing her appeal, Veronica was called into an executive session in which one of the studio heads said her salary would be boosted from $75 to $500 a week. Most actresses would have leapt into the studio boss's lap and at least have kissed his forehead in gratitude. Not Veronica. She stonily argued, "To hell with it. I get a thousand dollars a week from now on or nothing." She stormed out of the office afterward and refused to discuss the matter further. Well, she didn't get the $1,000, but the studio did compromise with $750—nearly ten times her previous weekly salary. For the moment, Veronica was satisfied.

Paramount's stolid regime of cigar-chomping executives knew it was not fair remuneration, since Veronica was fast becoming one of Hollywood's hottest commodities. They also knew that the trademark long bob of golden blond hair slipping over one eye was turning into a fantastic publicity gimmick. Press releases flooded the country's leading newspapers and magazines, each revealing specific measurements and little known facts about Veronica's honey-colored hair. The "Lake Look," as it was called, became the most requested style in the nation's beauty salons, where women were offered imitation Veronica Lake hairstyles for a reasonable price. *Life* magazine ran a full-page spread on this newest hairdo craze, while Paramount's press corp continued to conjure up new nicknames in frequent press releases. These included "Detour Coiffure" and "Peeping Pompadour," but the one the public most identified her with was "Peekaboo."

Clearly Lake's hairdo also helped boost morale in America and helped take everyone's minds off the continuing world war in Europe. According to the *Life* magazine article, Veronica's wavy hairline included about 150,000 hairs, each measuring about 0.00023 in cross section, with the locks 17 inches in front, 24 inches in back, and falling about 18 inches below her shoulder.

Although Veronica originally wore her hair short, she started liking the change because there was less wear and tear when it was long. To maintain its beauty, she usually brushed it fifteen minutes a day and washed it twice each morning in Nulava shampoo and once in Maro oil, before rinsing it in vinegar. At first, Veronica was frankly amazed at all the publicity her hair had garnered. In fact, when she was first placed under contract at Paramount, both Dorothy

Lamour and Patricia Morrison had more hair on their heads than she ever had. Off screen, Veronica could easily conceal her identity by simply doing her hair up in braids or hiding it under a turban.

Veronica's extreme peekaboo bob soon inspired more jokes than any single subject until the appearance of the Edsel. Within months of her successful screen debut, top-flight radio comedians and newspaper columnists began relying on her topical coiffure for show-stopping material. Lou Costello, of the Abbott and Costello team , once suggested that "Veronica should push back her hair and open up a second front." Bob Hope quipped, "Veronica Lake wears her hair over one eye because it's a glass eye." Groucho Marx, hosting radio's *You Bet Your Life,* spouted, "I opened my mop closet the other day and I thought Veronica Lake fell out." Reporting on war activities overseas, Walter Winchell wrote: "Norway dangles on the map like Veronica Lake's hair." And the pièce de résistance: on Fred Allen's show, after a cop stopped him for having only one headlight, the officer said to Allen, "Hey, what you trying to pull . . . a Veronica Lake?"

Veronica took these jokes good-naturedly, seeing these rounds of innocent barbs as compliments. She had indeed arrived.

In an interview around this time with newspaper columnist Erskine Johnson, Lake remarked that the constant press attention over her famous coiffure had finally begun to bore her. She complained: "Some darn cartoonist even had a silly dame who was supposed to be twice as glamourous as I am. She had her hair down in front of both eyes. But did you see what happened when she had her hair cut? Well, she looked like this." Veronica pushed out her ears like Clark Gable (known for his oversized ears), then crossed her eyes and said, "I was just awful."

Perhaps what turned Veronica off was the fact her hairdo had become more of a fad than her trademark. Even Teet Carle agrees: "Angles for stories and stunts seemed to drop into our hands with almost yawning simplicity. I'll admit that the one-eyed gimmick got twisted to the point of nausea and that even we created and fed out ideas of our own to the press to capitalize on it."

But Paramount did its best not to overexpose Veronica. Executives contemplated what to do next with their prize star, but they were in no hurry. Two roles were submitted for consideration, one as the lead in Kitti Fring's *Blonde Venus* and the other in *China Pass*. With nothing else left for her, Paramount decided instead to cast Veronica in a low-budget quickie, *Hold Back the Dawn,* which was released on September 26, 1941.

This film utilized some unused footage of Richard Webb and Veronica performing a telephone musical number that was originally shot for *I Wanted Wings,* but had been cut in the final editing. Veronica then appeared in some new footage opposite Charles Boyer, the film's star, who tries selling director Mitch Leisen (playing a film director named Mr. Saxon) on directing a screen version of his life story. Arthur Hornblow, Jr. also produced this film.

Unfortunately, Veronica's performance, which was unbilled, received no mention in reviews. It certainly would have helped, since the picture went on to receive favorable reviews from every critic in the country.

As she found out eventually, however, someone was keeping close watch on her. At the studio around this time, Preston Sturges was making a name for himself as one of Hollywood's greatest screwball comedy directors. Sturges, only forty-three, was extremely multitalented for his age: he wrote, produced, and directed his films, and was soon labeled "a starmaker" for his genius for molding young unknowns into stars.

Sturges was involved in the preproduction planning of a satirical comedy, *Sullivan's Travels*, which he was writing, producing, and directing. Preston had already signed Joel McCrea for the lead role of an underprivileged film director turned hobo, and he wanted Veronica to play opposite McCrea as his nameless roadside companion, "The Girl." Other co-stars included Robert Warwick, William Demarest, and Franklin Pangborn.

Preston had come to Paramount on the heels of directing an acclaimed New York stage show called *Bad Girl.* His deft style of comedy direction had bolted him to the top, winning the attention of Paramount and other studios, and Paramount won out. He was given an exclusive contract, his own production company, complete control of his films, and his private booth in the studio's commissary. Contract player Julie Gibson, formerly Sturges' confidant and co-star of *Hail the Conquering Hero,* recalls that Sturges' personality often intimidated others. "Preston was a lionesque, tall, massive man, with a generous sized moustache, and beautiful green eyes. He had enough ego that he had caricatures, cartoons, and photographs of himself all over the walls of his office around a gigantic desk. When you walked in, you were impressed. And he was a charmer."

Richard Webb, who also worked with Sturges in *Sullivan's Travels,* provided his own insights: "Preston was a flamboyant type of character with a great sense of humor and his entire concentration was on making his films great epics. He had a shyness about him, which is why Veronica may have liked him, but when he was at work, he had a typically big smile that would open up the world."

Gibson also remembers that there was a definite shyness about Sturges, which she believes equaled Veronica's own reserve. But, unlike Veronica, Sturges surrounded himself with his own legion of "yes-men." Gibson also said that Sturges had his own stock method of selecting the different actresses for his films, and that he used the same approach in snatching up Veronica. As she recalls:

> I know Preston did the same thing with Veronica. He had his own table, a big baronial one in the commissary, and he would sit at the head of it with his back to the wall so he could see everyone who came in to the commissary. Many times this was how he would pick his talent. He would see the young, new hopefuls the studio had signed and check them out with the talent department. He found out who the person was, what they'd done, what their background was, and then called them into his office for an interview, before casting them into one of his pictures. I know that he spotted Veronica the same way, and saw something in her, a quality that not even the heads of the studio or talent department had noticed.

That quality was Veronica's ability to play straight comedy. Paramount was reluctant to assign Veronica to Sturges for *Sullivan's Travels* because they felt she was too clearly established as "a movie heavy" from acting in too many serious roles. One studio executive protested, "One smile from her [Veronica] and the lens will crack." But Sturges vehemently disagreed. It took hours of deliberating and negotiating with Paramount executives before Sturges convinced them that Veronica was right for the part. Sturges tested three other girls and screened the final filmed tests for the executives. All agreed that Lake stood hair and shoulders above the others. The part was hers.

In an interview, Sturges once voiced his enthusiasm over Veronica's screen presence, comparing her to some of

Hollywood's legends. As he said: "Veronica's one of the great little people, like Mary Pickford, Douglas Fairbanks, and Freddie Bartholomew, who took hold immediately with their audiences. She was nothing much in real life—a quiet, rather timid little thing—but the screen transformed her, electrified her, and brought her to life."

Sturges repeatedly said that Veronica's sudden rise from obscurity to stardom was also because she was like "a child of the camera." He added: "Miss Lake was born to be photographed. Photographed from any angle, with any type of lighting from candle to giant searchlight, she looks perfect. She is one of the most photogenic subjects the screen has ever known. She belongs in front of the camera."

Soon after Veronica was signed for *Sullivan's Travels*, Sturges invited her into his office to discuss her involvement in the picture. He sketched a dress pattern for the costume he wanted Veronica to wear in the film. It wasn't unusual for Sturges to sketch costume roughs for each of his films. Although the final decision usually rested upon the extremely capable shoulders of Edith Head, who was the head of costuming, Sturges always delivered his ideas on paper to Head first.

Veronica was clearly satisfied with the way in which Sturges had been treating her: like a queen. Preston had even made a point of keeping her informed throughout the long, drawn-out negotiations he had with the studio to win her. He would call her every day with an update, telling her each time to "keep a stiff upper lip." Veronica became very fond of Preston because, like her, he was basically insecure, reserved, and shy. But Veronica lacked Preston's ability to confront her problems openly. Without any psychiatric treatment, her phobia about people continued to deepen.

This was further illustrated before *Sullivan's Travels*

went into production. The same day she learned she was going to star in the film, she also received news of a more personal nature. She was pregnant. Veronica believed that John got her pregnant the last day of filming *I Wanted Wings*, but she didn't realize it until she started having dizzy spells. Naturally, she was deathly afraid to tell Sturges because she feared Paramount would drop her from the film entirely. So, she didn't tell anyone.

John was far from elated. He had never wanted children because of the responsibility. But Veronica did, and she never used any birth control devices as she had promised. The least pleased was Veronica's mother, still distraught over her daughter's secret marriage. When Veronica broke the news over the phone, Constance violently remarked, "What are you trying to do, ruin your career? Think of what you've worked for. How could you?" Constance was short on words for the first time. Doctors had always told Constance that her daughter's major vulnerability—another characteristic of her schizophrenia—would be her inability to mother her children, but this Veronica never knew.

Unable to tell the truth, however (to her mother, and perhaps even to herself), Veronica retorted, "John is the one who kept insisting that we have a baby. What do you want from me?"

Veronica tried to remain aloof during the conversation, but broke down. Half-believing her daughter, and very upset, Constance asked, "Where's John now? Let me talk to him." John wasn't there, but that evening when he returned, Constance called again to talk to him. She said, "You should have thought about this more carefully, John."

John just listened. Meanwhile, Veronica slumped in her chair, waiting to hear how her husband would defend her. She came undone at the seams when John finally retorted, "Well, it's not my fault. Veronica wanted the baby."

In one swift blurry motion, Veronica leaped to her feet, put on her coat, grabbed her handbag, and stormed over to Rita Beery's house, her next-door neighbor and the former wife of actor Wallace Beery. When she finally returned home with a cooler head two days later, she was still upset. Veronica was well aware that it took two to tango, but she didn't want to admit her responsibility. But for the time being, she accepted her plight.

When *Sullivan's Travels* commenced filming on May 13, 1941, three months before the baby was due, rumors began spilling out of the Paramount compound that Veronica was expecting. She quickly denied these rumors as "merely speculation." But during the production of *Sullivan's Travels* Veronica, for the first time since her screen test, found it difficult to be natural in front of the cameras. Sturges noticed that she was better unprepared for her scenes than overprepared, and finally instructed her, "Don't ever walk on my set knowing anything about your lines or scenes." Veronica gave stiffer réadings when she overrehearsed and thus wasn't able to rise above her own expectations in playing her scenes. He was right.

Veronica later stated in an interview: "I didn't prepare for the rest of the film and for most of the films I worked in afterwards. *Sullivan's Travels* was one of the great moviemaking experiences of my career, and Sturges was simply a genius. The word got around town that I was better without so much preparation, and most directors [after that] accepted and worked with it."

Sullivan's Travels also made other news firsts for Veronica. Although she kept her beautiful locks of hair tucked under a cap and her figure under wraps during filming, Veronica revealed her legs to film audiences for the very first time. Teet Carle says such gimmicks were to the definite advantage of Paramount's press agents when promoting Veronica. "Every time Veronica changed her hairdo it was worth a story. In *Sullivan's Travels,* her legs were actually shown for the very first time and it also marked the first time she wore a bathing suit on film. Newspapers ran gobs of photos happily showing that she had good gams."

Veronica might have had good gams, but her pregnancy became increasingly apparent. She didn't want to upset Sturges, but knew that she had to tell him eventually. A week into filming, Sturges' wife, Louise, and actress Mary Martin paid a visit to the set. Spectators on the sidelines, Louise and Mary, both pregnant themselves, were happily discussing how much they looked forward to their respectful newborns. Preston jokingly called them "the stork club," never realizing that Veronica was soon to become member number three.

Although Veronica rarely mingled on the set, she made an exception this time and went over to chat with Louise. Keenly aware of her loner image, Louise was surprised by Veronica's sudden outgoingness, but turned remarkably grim when Veronica whispered into her ear: "Please don't tell Preston, but I'm also pregnant." Louise flatly stated, "He has to know, Veronica. You have to tell him . . . and now."

Shaking in her shoes, Veronica walked up to Sturges, tapped him on the shoulder, then quietly dropped the bomb. "There's something I have to tell you," she said. "I won't be able to work indefinitely. I'm going to have a baby." Sturges just buckled over with laughter. As Teet Carle recounts: "Everybody was afraid at what his response would be, that maybe he'd feel as if he had been had. But when he found out, he just leaned back in his director's chair and laughed his goddamn head off. Any girl who could put something over ol' Preston had achieved quite a feat. He said, 'Don't worry about it, Veronica, we'll work everything out.' "

Actually, according to Teet Carle, Veronica had gone to see Edith Head earlier in the morning for advice. As soft-spoken as the actress, Head was like a second mother to Veronica. During their conversation, Head assured Veronica that she could design some baggy clothing to help conceal her pregnancy, but added, "I'm not going to help you with anything else; you tell Preston the truth and that you and I have talked everything out."

News of Veronica's pregnancy created a furor among Paramount's executive staff; in fact, a special board meeting was called to determine whether she could continue working in the film. Supposedly, one executive groaned, "Here we are publicizing her as a glamour girl and she has to have a baby!" Another executive just cupped his hands and buried his head in total disbelief. But, after consulting Lake's family doctor, Paramount's power structure agreed to keep Veronica on. It was also then that Sturges revealed Edith Head's plan to costume her in baggy clothing, and his strategy to film her in a variety of back and side shots from the waist up.

Veronica once explained her reason for secrecy: "I just couldn't afford to take the six months off, so I worked. I worked right up until a week before Elaine was born. The final thing I did was take a portrait sitting, which didn't have much to do with acting, admittedly, but I wanted to cooperate as far as I could right up to the last minute."

That is only part of the story. Veronica also kept quiet about her pregnancy because she didn't want the baby. As with most female schizophrenics, she anticipated the birth of her child with joy initially, but eventually came to resent the idea. As a result, whenever anybody asked her about the baby, she frequently went out of her way to be nasty toward them. At the time, nobody on the set could understand her sudden behavioral change. She had never made much of an effort to be sociable, but now she was often openly antagonistic. According to Veronica's mother, her daughter even thought seriously about having an abortion. "Veronica didn't want children. When she was first pregnant with Elaine, she came to the house one night and said to me, 'I'll have an abortion if you want me to.' I said, 'I didn't ask you to have an abortion.' I think she knew that, because it was obvious that *she* wanted the abortion. But she never did."

Veronica became so despondent over her pregnancy that her attitude prompted one executive to observe, "She wasn't such a bad girl, she was just having horns."

In a matter of days, crew members began handling Veronica with kid gloves, doing everything possible to make her feel comfortable. Whenever any scenes were too risky, Sturges replaced Veronica with a stunt double named Cheryl Walker, formerly the 1938 Rose Bowl Queen, who substituted for Lake in several of her films. During one scene, Veronica and Joel McCrea were scheduled to frolic in an oversized swimming pool at a private Hollywood mansion, which the studio was renting for the movie.

In the script, Veronica was to push McCrea with all of his clothes on into the pool head first. Then, while straddling the pool's edge and telling him off, McCrea would pull Veronica legs first into the water, in sort of playful revenge. But Walker was inserted into the scene at the last minute. Mixing fantasy with reality, when the stunt was finished Veronica dove into the sparkling water with McCrea, pregnant and all. Caught by surprise, Preston turned the cameras on and began filming the scene over. Joel repeated many of the same antics with Veronica that he had masterfully performed with Walker, even pushing her underwater. But after being shoved beneath the surface, Veronica didn't resurface. Her petticoat had become twisted awkwardly over her head, causing her to bob helplessly to the top of the water. Joel quickly released her from the petticoat, carried her in his arms, and laid her on the grass outside the pool, deeply concerned, as Veronica was in her eighth month of pregnancy. Clearly upset, Sturges, hovering over Veronica like her guardian angel, growled, "That was a pretty dumb stunt, Veronica."

Still gasping for air, she said wearily, "I know, but it looked so refreshing. I just couldn't resist."

In the midst of the commotion, Sturges summoned the studio doctor to the scene to check Veronica over thoroughly. Fortunately, no damage was done to her or the baby. Realizing Veronica was going to recover from her near drowning, Sturges ordered her to report back after lunch to film some additional poolside scenes.

In remembering the aftermath of the pool incident, Teet Carle says, "Veronica caused some heart attacks that afternoon by diving in. But that was Veronica, the tomboy, pure and simple. She was eternally living in a world of childish fantasy."

6
...

A Little Fluff
Can Go a Long Way

VERONICA REALLY COULDN'T
HELP living in her Walter Mittyish dream world. It was safer
than the real world and it created fewer dilemmas for her.
Even if anyone could have persuaded her to seek psychiatric help, schizophrenia is extremely difficult to treat. Only
those who knew her intimately noticed that she reveled in
childish reveries, and thus, cloaked herself in a shroud of
unpredictability and mystique.

According to her cousin Helene, Veronica hated the
formality of reporters interviewing her on her private life
and personal interests. To keep them always guessing,
she never gave these journalists the same answer twice.
If she was asked what her favorite meal was, she might
answer "spaghetti," and two days later give an entirely
different response. She was often whimsical and just
couldn't resist playing childlike, prankish schemes during
these interviews. Veronica treated the reporters' con-

stant barrage of questioning as just another game to play.

Although happy enough with her own distortions, Veronica had a great disdain for the fairy-tale material press agents often dreamed up for her studio biographies and for syndicated newspaper columnists. Just one among many, Sidney Skolsky, a famous newspaper biographer of movie stars, often made Veronica a subject in his column. Due to her sex-kitten image, some material he used tugged on the heartstrings of male filmgoers, creating what men perceived as "the perfect girl." In one article, Skolsky claimed: "She collects perfume bottles and has no personal preferences. She just likes to smell good. Veronica also prefers baths to showers, especially bubble baths as she likes to linger in the tub and relax. She *hates* to dry herself thoroughly and pats herself with a thick towel. She sleeps in a nightgown with the windows open and reads before falling asleep."

Close but no cigar, according to Teet Carle, who admits: "We dreamed up most of that stuff. It was all part of hyping an image." Certainly Skolsky's description underscores what Paramount wanted readers to remember about Veronica: that she was as sensual off screen as on. But the real Veronica was rather different than the woman portrayed by studio publicity. It was true that she was a smoker (although not a chain-smoker) and enjoyed nightclubs (contrary to what the studio reported). She was very suspicious of people who tried to become friendly with her in a day. Her favorite book was Walt Whitman's *Leaves of Grass*, and Chinese red was her favorite color in clothing and furnishings.

She also staged her share of Hollywood hoaxes. Like most stars, she was often likely to embroider the facts of her life, especially when it suited one of her delusions. For example, when someone once asked her place of birth, she said Lake Placid. Her reason: "I was wrong. I know it, but somehow Lake Placid sounded so much more romantic a place to be born than Brooklyn."

Veronica also created other fantasies about her still young life. Teet Carle explains:

> Veronica was always living in a world of fantasy, and would say anything that came to her head. And it always sounded for real. Because of the honesty of her angelic face, she made it all sound very genuine. I remember hearing her talk knowledgeably about flying, fiction, the military, horseracing, music, archery, art, or whatnot, adding that she was an expert in the subject. Once she enthralled a man for an hour, describing with utter reality her personal oil painting. She never knew that he taught art at a local college, but it wouldn't have mattered to her. The bottom line was that she never studied any of these subjects, but she had such a vivid imagination that she could fool anyone.

Jack Hirshberg, who wrote a syndicated Hollywood column for forty Canadian newspapers, was another of Veronica's victims. Hirshberg had moved his office to Hollywood to be closer to the celebrity scene. After he had been in Los Angeles for about a year, his editor at the *Montreal Standard* heard reports that Veronica Lake was born in Montreal, raised at a nearby convent, and attended McGill University's famous medical school. Because of the local angle, Hirshberg was assigned to the story. But, as he recalls today, it turned out to be a put on, and Veronica was at the root of the problem:

> McGill University was one of the finest medical schools on the continent. My father happened to be a doctor in Montreal, so I was familiar with the school and everybody there. Well, word had gotten around

that Veronica had attended McGill. She supposedly described to someone her two years as a pre-med student there and how the head of the medical department, Dr. Archibald, took her hands in his and said, "My dear, you have the hands of a great surgeon." Well, this was a nice angle for the Montreal paper and she went into considerable detail, so I wrote it up and the paper ran the story complete with photographs. Well, afterwards all hell broke loose. Someone at McGill searched their files and records and couldn't come up with anybody who had gone there under the name "Veronica Lake." I wasn't worried about that, because her name wouldn't have been Veronica Lake at the time, it would have been Constance Keane. So I told them to check Constance Keane. They did, but nobody had heard of Constance Keane, much less Dr. Archibald. So I was really in hot soup. My editors thought I sat and made the whole story up, and even threatened to bring suit against me, for what I don't know, since there weren't any damages. Luckily, she had told another version of that story to *Life* magazine, roughly around the same time. She told them enough to substantiate that what she had told me was pure fabrication.

After Hirshberg confronted Veronica with the falseness of the story, she agreed to straighten out the entire mess. As Hirshberg tells it: "The people at the studio had a talk with her and they decided to put her on a plane to Montreal, whereupon she would talk to Dr. Cyril James, who was the president of McGill University. So, I took her to the airport, I put her on the plane, and the next day in Montreal she told everybody that I had made the story up. That proved to be a real tip-off to the kind of person she was. As my editor told me later, 'Next time you interview a movie star, take along a lie detector.' "

What seemed more ironic, however, was that after the incident blew over, Hirshberg was hired to work in the Paramount publicity department. His first assignment was to cover Veronica for *I Wanted Wings*. But, according to Hirshberg, Veronica was uncooperative because she was afraid that he knew something about her that she didn't want known. "I received no cooperation from her at all. She was circulating all sorts of crap in order to get me fired, because she didn't feel comfortable with me since I knew what kind of person she was. Of course, she wasn't able to get me fired, but I don't remember her very kindly for it. She ultimately got what she very richly deserved in the end."

Finally, order was restored with the McGill University faculty when Veronica's mother followed her daughter's trip with one of her own. "I went up and straightened that out, blaming the entire incident on the Paramount publicity department. The president thanked me, but only later did I find out that Veronica's mouth had got her in trouble."

Veronica's unpredictability surfaced again during the making of *Sullivan's Travels*. Richard Webb recalls that Veronica had been asked to report to Teet Carle's office right away. As Webb recounts:

When Veronica had a Mona Lisa-enigmatic smile on her face, you never knew what the girl was thinking. The studio certainly didn't know what to do with her because *they* didn't know what she was thinking. For instance, Louella Parsons once asked Teet Carle, Paramount's head of publicity, to help arrange a luncheon interview with Veronica. Parsons was the biggest columnist at that time, and everybody was scared to death of her because of the power that she wielded in the press. Well, Veronica met with Louella in Carle's office, and Teet said, "Louella would like to have lunch with you, and interview you." Now, Louella looked just like a frog . . . just like a frog the way she was dressed. So when Veronica looked at her, she first curled her lip and then said, 'Well, I don't mind the interview, but do I have to *eat* with her?'

Fortunately, Parsons gave Veronica a good write-up in her column and that, perhaps, because Veronica was gutsy enough to stand up to her, which few people did.

Veronica continued to surprise everyone with her unexpected antics on the set as well. On one occasion, a Canadian journalist was interviewing Preston Sturges in French, with Sturges replying in the same language. When asked to explain Veronica's many screen qualities, Preston suddenly experienced great difficulty in remembering how to say in French, "She's the envy of most American women." Veronica, who had gone to school (but not as a pre-med student) in Montreal, could still speak French rather fluently and came to Preston's rescue, ticking off the sentence which Preston had such problems remembering, in correct French. Sturges and the reporter stood there in disbelief as Veronica strolled away.

Lake was also forgetful of appointments and was rarely punctual when it came to making personal appearances or keeping luncheon dates, unless she was with an escort. Several examples of her tardiness have been chronicled, including the time Veronica kept a friend from the studio waiting two hours for a luncheon date. Her excuse: "The bus was late." (Veronica never rode the bus in her life.)

Veronica's unreliability often discouraged even her creditors, including Preston Sturges. Sturges, who operated a dinner nightclub off screen, reported that Veronica owed more than fifty dollars for dinners she had eaten there. As Preston once recalled: "The manager wrote letters and tried to get her on the telephone a dozen times, but she never paid any attention to him. She was very spoiled, I guess."

Helene Nielsen sees two reasons for her peculiar behavior: "Veronica didn't want people staring at her all the time and was happy in her own little world. She didn't like all this exposure, and was very shy to begin with. She forgot her appointments because she was either too tired or wrought emotionally with her personal matters, which got her so wound up that she'd say, 'Hey, look I have to rest and take care of things for myself!' " Nielsen also points out that Veronica didn't know how to deal with all the public adulation, nor with her own emotions. Thus, by retreating to her own private shell, she felt protected from any outside dangers.

Veronica also admitted to her lack of punctuality, but she provided another reason for it: "I admit I'm a complete moron about hours and that I literally never know what time it is. I have watches and clocks all around me and never see them. When I get doing one thing, whether it's eating, or fitting clothes, or discussing politics, I never can seem to remember that I must go on, at some particular hour, and do something else."

The public expected Veronica to appear the same as she did on the screen: exotic, sexy, bigger than life. Most fans expected her to be taller and were totally unprepared when confronted with her minute proportions, which included an eighteen-inch waist. She always appeared much larger on film than she actually was. In fact, some have said that she was the shortest siren in the business, shorter than either Theda Bara or Hedy Lamarr. She only stood five feet one inch, and weighed ninety-eight pounds at the height of her career.

She managed to turn some heads in her time, though, as Constance attests: "Bette Davis wrote in her autobiography that 'Veronica Lake was the most beautiful person who ever came to Hollywood.' She was right. I mean, you'd walk down Sunset Boulevard and people from everywhere would turn around and look at her. She was very unassuming. In fact, we used to call her 'Gertie Glamour.' "

But Veronica was unprepared for the public's reaction. In an interview, she once confessed: "I've always been a simple person, with simple tastes. I much prefer daytime sports to nightclub dancing. I love horseback riding, hunting, fishing, swimming, all that, and I'd rather eat a hamburger than pheasant under [glass] any time. I'm much more comfortable in slacks and no makeup than sequined down and in full war paint."

On August 21, l941, a month after *Sullivan's Travels* was completed, Veronica was admitted to Good Samaritan Hospital, where she gave birth that same day to a daughter, Elaine. Fortunately, Veronica experienced no complications during labor, and John was at her bedside following delivery. Flowers from her many associates lined her hospital room, including one very lavish bouquet from Preston Sturges and his wife. Veronica had always considered herself an unwanted child, and she felt the same about Elaine. During her pregnancy, Veronica had been ambivalent about having a child. Now looking at her newborn daughter, she realized that the extra responsibilities of raising her would be far more taxing than she had imagined.

Elaine was strikingly beautiful for a newborn baby. She had her mother's pert nose, but otherwise didn't resemble Veronica very much, being dark-haired with dark blue eyes.

John, who had not wanted children, accepted the added responsibility enthusiastically. He handed out cigars to members of the hospital staff, and following the delivery he was so excited that he called Teet Carle. Carle was preparing to leave on vacation at the time with his wife and children. As he recalls: "We were going to leave early Friday night to get an early start. Just as we were getting ready to leave, the phone rang. It was John Detlie on the phone, saying that Veronica had had this baby girl. He was so high, so thrilled, that he said, 'Another future motion picture star.' He told me all about the birth and then I had to sit down, postpone my trip temporarily, call all the newspapers and wire services."

Bedridden for several weeks, Veronica returned home from the hospital and tried to regain her stamina. She clearly wanted to go back to work again. With Elaine now a part of the family, however, she took a long hiatus from the film world to put her life in order first.

At about this time, John and Veronica bought a small home in Mandeville Canyon, which was near Santa Monica and east of where her parents were living. They turned one of the rooms into a private nursery for Elaine, complete with the usual kaleidoscope of baby toys. John seemed to like his new role of father and played with his newborn daughter often, making funny faces until she laughed uncontrollably. Another pleasant change had also taken place in Veronica's life: her mother, who had been angry over Veronica's surprise pregnancy, accepted her granddaughter with open arms. She was delighted with Elaine and resumed her friendship with John.

But in 1941, the world itself was becoming an unsafe place. World War II was in high gear and following the invasion of Pearl Harbor on December 7, 1941, the United States mobilized for full-scale war. Hollywood soon began supporting the war by producing a succession of war films and propaganda short subjects.

It was during this bleak period in American history that

Veronica's popularity really soared. With millions of Americans at war, many of these soldiers needed a girl they could call their own. Veronica became *that* girl to these servicemen, who pasted photos of her on barrack walls or carried clippings of her in their wallets. One air force squadron even named their B-29 after her. Veronica had always felt uneasy about being idolized, but she viewed this new relationship with American servicemen as more of a patriotic honor than a personal compliment.

At this point, filmgoers hadn't seen Veronica on the screen for almost half a year. Not many remembered her last film, *Hold Back the Dawn,* but they were being constantly reminded through a flood of publicity about her next release, *Sullivan's Travels.* The film made its nationwide premiere on January 28, 1942, at the Paramount Theatre in midtown New York. Streams of moviegoers jammed the Paramount lobby on opening night, pushing and shoving to find seats. It wasn't your typical film premiere complete with scores of Hollywood celebrities arriving in chauffeur-driven limousines. Paramount did not go in for splashy promotions with their films in the 1940s, unless it was for an epic like *Gone With the Wind.* Nevertheless, fans weren't disappointed.

Sullivan's Travels paired Joel McCrea and Veronica for the first time. They were not only adorable to watch but their performances won countless critical plaudits. Billed second in the film, Veronica scored her third straight victory with critics in this, her first comedy performance. In her three-star rated New York *Daily News* review, critic Kate Cameron enthused: "Veronica fulfills the promise she gave in *I Wanted Wings* by giving a first-rate performance." *Newsweek,* also obsessed with her conversion to a comedienne, observed: "Now Sturges swaddles her principal asset in a hobo's outfit, stuffs her hair under a disreputable cap and reveals for the first time the lady has two profiles and decided possibilities as an actress." *Sullivan's Travels* would become Veronica's most remembered film; she had turned in a performance she found tough to equal during her career.

After the film's overwhelming success, and much to her chagrin, Paramount chose not to star her in any more comedies for an indefinite period of time even though she enjoyed making them. As her cousin Helene relates: "I think the reason she liked comedy was because she was out of her shell. She had to get out of that shell she was in, and escape the pressures. And comedy put her in that happier world." But Paramount remained adamant: she would do as she was told, or else. . . .

Veronica was given another fling at comedy, however, when she reprised her role from *Sullivan's Travels* for CBS' *Lux Radio Theatre*. Ralph Bellamy substituted for Joel McCrea, and the program went on the air on November 9, 1942. It was Veronica's second appearance on the program —her first broadcast had featured her in the starring role in *I Wanted Wings*. But, according to Helene, Veronica felt very nervous and uncomfortable on live radio. The spontaneous dissemination of these programs unraveled her, but despite her phobia, she never made any mistakes. As Nielsen recalls: "Veronica didn't like radio because she was just reading cold from a script and wasn't reacting to anybody, like you do in a filmed scene. I think she reacted better to actors who gave her feedback than she did to sound effects they used in radio. Sometimes it was a little frightening. She'd be wondering, 'Am I sounding all right?' With movies, you could see the rushes and do them over. But it scared her that as she talked she was being heard, leaving little room for mistakes."

Shortly before the release of *Sullivan's Travels,*

Veronica received the news that *The Harvard Lampoon,* a nationally published college humor magazine, had singled her out as one of Hollywood's "six worst stars." Veronica was listed as "the worst discovery of the year," Betty Grable as turning in "the year's consistently worst performance," Jeanette MacDonald as "the most unattractive actress," Rudy Vallee as the singer of "the most nauseating song" ("As If You Didn't Know"), and Nelson Eddy and Alice Faye as moving "fastest on the downward path."

Veronica had no comment on the selection.

To her later dismay, however, *Sullivan's Travels* was the last time she worked under Preston Sturges. They remained good friends around the studio, socializing occasionally off screen. Preston always maintained the highest praise for her work. He certainly knew how to handle her and would have surely enhanced her career had he directed her again. But Paramount's top brass would never hear of such a thing, as Julie Gibson, one of Sturges' closest friends, explains: "A lot of people Preston had discovered at Paramount eventually fell by the wayside because nobody else knew how to handle them. I always felt Veronica was one of them. Had Preston made one or two more pictures with her, he could have controlled her destiny. He knew how to control her and he knew how to show her off to her best advantage, something which Paramount didn't know anything about."

But Veronica had to serve out her Paramount contract, and Helene Nielsen agreed that Veronica was harmed by the way she was being improperly managed. As she observes: "There isn't any doubt in my mind that Preston would have been good for Veronica. They both understood each other. She needed someone like him, since he really cared about her and would have guided her. Instead, she got stuck with the kind of people who didn't understand her."

Nielsen didn't elaborate or name any individuals, but they probably ranged from the studio hierarchy down to the talent department. Veronica never spoke ill publicly about her so-called "enemies," but privately she was convinced they existed. Edith Head was Veronica's closest friend at the studio. She stood close to Lake and supported and comforted her whenever she got caught up in some kind of trouble. Most believe, however, that Veronica's "enemy list" was another self-destructive delusion. Veronica was the victim of her own emotional fragility. She imagined situations, or magnified the slightest hint of criticism of her: many times the hurts and hostility she felt simply never existed. Mixing that paranoia with reality, she gradually began to believe that such problems were developing all around her. At such times, Veronica would retreat even further inside herself, sometimes practically hiding from those on the set who had to be in close contact with her.

To compound her problems, John felt that Veronica wasn't adequately handling her responsibilities to Elaine, that he was carrying more than his share. Her career was taking precedent over her roles as mother and wife. And John didn't like being left behind. Whenever they attended Hollywood gatherings, Veronica and John were invariably introduced as "Mrs. Veronica Lake and John Detlie." But though it was usual for the star to be mentioned first at these functions, John never felt it was acceptable in the case of man and wife. His own frustrations only hardened in the months and years ahead—a clash between him and Veronica seemed inevitable.

Left: Veronica, age 18 months, with nursemaid. *(credit: Constance Keane)*

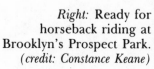

Right: Ready for horseback riding at Brooklyn's Prospect Park. *(credit: Constance Keane)*

At age eight, Veronica strikes a peekaboo pose on Miami Beach.
(credit: Jeff Lenburg Collection)

Left: Veronica, dressed as a western cowgirl, in Miami, Florida. *(credit: Constance Keane)*

Below: A young Veronica pictured during her Villa Maria Convent School days. *(credit: Jeff Lenburg Collection)*

Lake following her victory as Miss Miami. She was only sixteen.
(credit: Jeff Lenburg Collection)

Above: Hollywood bound: Helene Nielsen *(second from left, back row)*; Constance Keane *(third in back row)*; Veronica *(wearing hat)*; and Anthony Keane *(kneeling)*. *(credit: Helene Nielsen)*

Left: Veronica and her mother, Constance Keane, outside their Beverly Hills apartment. *(credit: Constance Keane)*

Below: Backstage at the Bliss-Hayden School of Acting. *(credit: Constance Keane)*

An early MGM portrait as Constance Keane. (*credit: Richard Webb*)

Above: Veronica in a cameo appearance in *All Women Have Secrets.* She was billed as Constance Keane. *(credit: Jeanne Cagney)*

Above: An August 1943 photograph showing Anthony Keane with granddaughter, Elaine, and stepdaughter, Veronica. *(credit: Constance Keane)*

Right: Husband John Detlie, with his daughter, Elaine. *(credit: Constance Keane)*

A young Alan Ladd with Veronica in *This Gun for Hire*.

7

. . .

Teaming With Alan Ladd

*I*T FRIGHTENED JOHN TO THINK that Veronica was changing, that he was slowly losing her, that she was sinking deeper into her fantasy world. Veronica wanted to tell her husband how much she hated being a mother. But she didn't have the courage to say what was on her mind. Instead, she continued drinking heavily at home, mostly alone and in the seclusion of her room so that John wouldn't know.

Her problem drinking, however, was never a secret again after Veronica threw a by-invitation-only New Year's party at her parents' house for the cast and crew of *Sullivan's Travels*. It wasn't like Veronica to play hostess, but Veronica was completely unpredictable. Those attending the party were unaware of her drinking, except for a select few.

According to Helene Nielsen, Veronica's limit was

usually two drinks, but by this point in her life, she had surpassed that limit. After a few drinks she was completely out of control. As doctors had warned previously, alcohol would only advance her acts of dementia, with Veronica unaware of her actions the following day. Richard Webb, who didn't receive an invitation, spoke with one of the party guests who worked at Paramount the next day. Bob Lucky saw Veronica's drinking as a direct result of her personal anxieties. Webb recalls:

> Veronica's stepfather was coming down the home stretch with tuberculosis, and they had a New Year's party at her parents' place. I wasn't invited. I was told by Bob Lucky from Paramount that everybody was supposed to be quiet and stay out of her stepfather's room. That night, however, Veronica had been drinking and she led a snake dance right through his bedroom with everybody shouting and screaming. I heard that she hated her stepfather. Perhaps, she still loved her real father.

Paramount's rumor mill began circulating the story the next day that Veronica "hated her stepfather," and with each retelling, the story became more exaggerated. According to Veronica's mother the incident was true but with one added twist: "Yes, that did happen. All of a sudden she began to get a vulgar streak in her, which I could never understand. Because after she led that snake dance into his room, she then did a striptease in front of him and everybody." Whatever the reason, Veronica surely needed help.

It was later hypothesized that she was reacting to John's announcement of several months before that he had joined the army. Veronica didn't tell anybody, but, inwardly, she knew she couldn't survive without him. What really devastated Veronica, however, was the way in which he had told her the news.

About two weeks after Pearl Harbor, just at the time Veronica was starting a new picture with Alan Ladd, John calmly announced one night after dinner that they would be moving to Seattle since he had been drafted by the army. He was being assigned as a major with the Camouflage Division Army Engineering Corp at Fort Lewis in Seattle, Washington.

Veronica, clearly upset and hurt over his secrecy, said she wouldn't go with him. John wanted to go for two obvious reasons: to serve his country, but, more importantly, to gain a status equal to that of his wife's. Veronica wasn't keen on living on an army base or on a soldier's salary. Nor did she want to permanently give up Hollywood and her career. Had John asked her several years earlier, she would probably have complied. Now, however, she was too well-established to suddenly pack it all in. She enjoyed making films, and the money she earned, though it wasn't buying her happiness, was another incentive. Sadly, they were growing apart.

Recalling John's enlisted days, Veronica once said:

That was a heavy, heavy time. No use pretending otherwise. We had dinner with Edith Head, her husband Bill Ihnen, and Mr. and Mrs. Preston Sturges that evening that he enlisted. John met us—we all came from the studio together—at the Players [Sturges' dinner nightclub]. He talked and laughed normally enough at dinner that I didn't suspect a thing. But immediately outside I knew by his wavering voice that something was wrong. When he told me what it was, tears began falling from my eyes. We were together as much as possible during the two weeks or so we had left. We went to our old haunting grounds. We visited the little hofbrau where we first danced to the "Beer Barrel Polka." We spent Sundays on the beach swimming and lying in the sun. And we drove to a little inn in the hills of Palos Verdes to be alone with our thoughts.

Emotions overcame Veronica, and loneliness and loss prevailed the night she bid John farewell, as she remembered:

I became really emotional when I walked John to the Los Angeles Union Train Station for the last time. We first stopped at a Mexican restaurant for our final dinner together. Then, afterwards, I walked him to his train and watched the train roll down the track in the midst of its own steam. I never had such an empty feeling. When I got home, I couldn't go in. I turned around and went over to visit with Edith Head and her husband, Bill, sitting with them for a while. I knew with the baby asleep and no John there that the house was going to seem as empty as a meeting hall.

Even if Veronica had wanted to go, she couldn't. A month earlier, Paramount had rushed her into another starring vehicle, a new thriller called *This Gun for Hire.* Based on the Graham Greene novel *A Gun for Sale,* Lake was being paired for the first time with a young, blond actor named Alan Ladd, who the studio was testing out as "a possible leading man."

Paramount executives would later realize the significance behind this "accidental piece of casting." The studio didn't like having Veronica inactive because they were losing money every minute she wasn't before the cameras, and, as fate would have it, nobody ever regretted the teaming of Ladd and Lake.

Alan Ladd, at 29, had been around Hollywood for nearly a decade, playing extra roles and an occasional bit part. He was three inches taller than Veronica: five feet four inches, an unusual height for a leading man. Adolph Zukor liked his leading men to be "tall, dark, and handsome, Tyrone Power-types," which Ladd wasn't. But Paramount had just lost the services of their blond box-office giant, Sterling Hayden, to the army and was fervently searching for a replacement. Ladd filled the bill, even though he wasn't as rugged looking. Like Veronica, Alan's diminutive size was also deceptive on the screen. Whenever he played opposite taller leading ladies, he stood either on a shoebox or on a stool to appear taller. *This Gun for Hire* never presented that problem, and it became more than just Ladd's first film with Veronica: It dramatically linked them in the public's mind as Hollywood's newest romantic team.

Paramount's executives did grumble, however, because they weren't able to turn Alan and Veronica into an off screen affair, not even for publicity. Veronica's housewife/mother image was too well-publicized by now; and Alan's agent (later his wife), Sue Carol, was very protective of her interest. If Veronica even shook hands with Ladd, she became very suspicious and hovered over her protégé like a hawk.

That's not to say that Veronica wasn't suspicious of Ladd. According to Teet Carle, she felt threatened by his presence, paranoid that he would upstage her:

> I remember telling Veronica, "I've seen the test of the guy who's going to be opposite of you." She said, "You mean, Robert Preston?" I said, "No, a chap named Alan Ladd. He's going to play the Raven." She said, "Oh. . . ." She just listened as I said, "Gee, he's sensational, too, Veronica. You'll like him." I didn't know whether I had gone overboard because she just

studied me for a while. You could tell she was disturbed. She had a good role, but as it turned out, Alan got probably more publicity and was featured more prominently in the film than she was.

Veronica later admitted the temptation of having an affair with Alan wasn't present, even though they both had similar personalities: he was quiet, introverted, lovable, and romantic. As she wrote in her autobiography, *Veronica*:

> Naturally, the public linked us romantically, but neither of us cared about what the public conjured up. And we were just as indifferent to the studio's sly attempts to spread romantic rumors. It was all part of the game in enticing the public into the theater, and the Ladd–Lake billing proved to be a powerful lure. In so many ways, we were kindred spirits. We were both professionally conceived through Hollywood's search for box office and the types to insure that box office. Both of us were also very aloof . . . we were a good match for another. It enabled us to work together very easily without friction or temperaments.

Richard Webb feels that Veronica and Alan were a worthy combination because "they both had a certain amount of delicacy about them." As he explains: "That's why Alan and Veronica worked so well together. They were both petite and perfectly formed, but there was no real substance to their relationship otherwise. Both reported to work and left on time, saying 'Hello,' and 'Good-bye' to each other. That was it."

Alan Ladd also spoke admirably of his first working relationship with Veronica. In an article, he remembered: "Although the atmosphere of the set was a bit impersonal because it was a low-budget picture, which had to be shot quickly, playing opposite Veronica Lake was an advantage to me. Until then, she had had mostly unsympathetic parts, and she was happy about this opportunity—eager to prove that she could portray the sympathetic character."

Yet, according to Richard Webb, Veronica never sought advice from Alan in playing a scene, and Ladd usually sought a second opinion from only one person: Sue Carol. She wielded her shield of power around the set, always speaking on Alan's behalf. As Webb tells it:

> Sue Carol *was* Alan Ladd. A director would cut a scene in which Alan was in and he'd say, "Cut." Alan would not look at the director afterwards, but at Sue. He'd go over and get the reading from her and come back and say, "Let's do it again." The director would reshoot the scene and say, "Cut," again. Alan would again look at Sue, and if the scene was okay by her, he'd say, "Okay, print that one." Veronica wasn't so selective. She usually did her scenes in one take, rarely blowing a line or reaction, while Alan was under the heavy-handed control of his wife, Sue Carol.

Sue never trusted Veronica, and the feelings were mutual. It wasn't until they had an opportunity to talk that they worked out their differences, as Teet Carle explains:

> I was always apprehensive about Sue Carol. She was a very hard woman to know. Alan was her whole life. And she was very jealous of him and zealous about his career. She was also jealous of Veronica. I thought if these two people ever clashed, it would have been very vicious. I know that Veronica always felt that many people didn't like her, which didn't help matters. Well, one night, Veronica's husband was going to pick her up. This was just before he went into the army. She

waited in the reception room out in front of the studio. For some reason, Sue left the set because Alan was still in his dressing room getting dressed. So she went out to the reception room. But Veronica was still waiting in the reception area, because Detlie was late. So, meanwhile, Sue sat down next to Veronica, they looked at each distrustingly, and then finally started talking to each other. They instantly won each other over, and became good friends afterwards. It was one of the great, beautiful things that happened to Veronica.

It was fortunate that Veronica and Sue became so close. Richard Webb recalls that Sue could be a powerful opponent. "I remember Sue called me up one day and wanted to have lunch with me. She said she wanted to represent me. I thought nothing of it, until some friend of mine called and said, 'Don't do it, she'll sign you up and do nothing with you.' What she was trying to do was become my agent so I would no longer be a a threat to Alan. But I declined."

Veronica felt differently about Frank Tuttle, her director, accusing him of using her in the film merely for "decorative purposes" and favoring Alan throughout the picture. Reportedly, she became very irritated when Tuttle began spending too much time filming scenes, in which she didn't appear, with Ladd. It is ironic that Tuttle treated her so sparingly since she was receiving top billing. The scars from this incident would never heal, and Veronica would later call Tuttle "a jerk who never considered me anything more than a sex-zombie whose only purpose in a movie was to cause mass masturbation and heavy breathing in darkened theaters."

As if it weren't enough to have Tuttle on her mind,

Veronica was also upset about her contract. According to Jan Grippo, who at this time became good friends with Veronica, she was still fuming over the fact she was earning only $750 a week as the studio's number one drawing card. Grippo, who later produced *The Bowery Boys* series, met Veronica on the set of *This Gun for Hire.* An established magician, Grippo was brought in by Tuttle to teach Veronica elementary legerdemain and how to perform sleight-of-hand card tricks in the film. On the contract dispute, Grippo recalls that "she was very unhappy with the contract. She projected that feeling, even though it wasn't known by everybody. She was only making $750 a week for being Paramount's number one star. That was like making $1,500 a week by today's standards, which was really nothing. I wish I could have handled her as an agent. I might have done better, I don't know. Our rapport was so good that I think I could have steered her right with her talents."

Veronica soon discovered, however, that Paramount operated under the laws of frugality when it came to signing and retaining its talent. The studio was under a three-man rule. B. G. "Buddy" DeSylva, a former Broadway producer and songwriter, headed the West Coast studio operation. Adolph Zukor, the studio's founding father, kept his nose out of DeSylva's business so long as he kept studio costs down. If he didn't, Zukor's right-hand man, Y. Frank Freeman, along with the studio president, Barney Balaban, would intervene. Each wielded an equal amount of power, and each had one primary concern: making and saving money. The studio was constantly signing and training young, attractive talent but at the lowest possible salaries. If some of them caught on, it would mean "a million dollar personality for pennies." If they didn't ignite, they were dropped after six months to a year at a minimal financial loss to the studio. Salaries for newcomers ranged from $150 to $300 a week, with raises negotiable at the end of the year. In recalling the studio's method of luring new talent, Julie Gibson (who was signed by Paramount in 1943) recalls that "they would sign up about twenty girls at a time every six months, hoping that one of them would show some talent. They signed them for a very minimum salary, but still, it was much better than you could get for doing anything else. The studio provided private lessons for acting, dancing, ballet, tap, singing, jazz, all for free, if you wanted to take advantage of them."

According to studio executives, Veronica's salary demands (she still wanted a $1,000 a week) were unreasonable and not in line with her potential. Lake's ongoing contract dispute further pointed up the studios' control. As Jan Grippo explains:

> All the studios were in control at the time. They were in control of contract players and people like Veronica, whipping them into shape. They paid you a small salary each week and worked you hard and maybe in too many pictures, but that was because they took advantage of your low salary and of the power that they had. They could suspend you so no other studio would hire you, if you didn't do what you were told. They could break your contract, or do a lot of other things. Now, the stars dominate the field. The star system has pretty much gone completely out of whack. At Paramount, though, they had means to keep these stars humble.

Grippo said that Veronica didn't stage any temper tantrums on the set while he was around, but she did vehemently discuss her problem. In his opinion, she knew better than to force a direct take-it-or-leave-it ultimatum. In fact, he was so impressed with her cooperation and professional ability that he contemplated forming a magic act with Veronica, but she later demurred. As he says, "It was true at the moment, but things happened. She was sincere about it, though."

Grippo added that what he admired most about Veronica was her perseverance, despite the personal problems she was suffering from at the time. In line with what others have said about her, he did say that "she deserved better. She was never treated right, or given the right opportunities."

Veronica experienced some lighter moments on the set of *This Gun for Hire* as well as with the film's romantic co-star, Robert Preston. Preston had the honor of giving Veronica her first screen kiss. Teet Carle remembers that Paramount's publicity department generated tons of publicity on that historic scene. According to Carle, Robert Preston found that scene most enjoyable. "I remember telling Bob, 'I want to shoot one good picture of you kissing Veronica.' He said glowingly, 'Well, okay, you really want something good!' I said, 'Yeah.' He said, 'Her eyebrows are going to curl then.' So they really clinched and kissed, and Veronica cried out, 'Whew . . . I'm sweating all over.' That was all in good fun, of course."

Veronica's private life, though, left something to be desired. She missed John, and when *This Gun for Hire* completed production, she immediately packed everything to join him in Seattle. As she later admitted, being "a camp follower" created its vast number of complications along the way. "My complications were different from those most girls would face. I convinced myself it would be madness to jeopardize a movie career by leaving Hollywood. But I also wanted to be with John."

But when Veronica joined John, she found that he had changed. Army life had made him tougher, more bull-headed, and in complete command. Thus, she found that her greatest challenge lay ahead: that of staying happily married to John.

8
. . .

The Star Machine

*1*942 WOULD BECOME the busi-
est year of Veronica's career. She would star in four top-
grossing films, achieve her greatest success on the screen
as Hollywood's number-one siren, and sell war bonds during a nationwide tour on behalf of Uncle Sam. And, she
would become a victim of Paramount's star machine. Once
they knew her value the studio overworked her and under-
paid her. Surprisingly, Veronica's mother refused to stick
her nose in this matter or to discuss her daughter's paltry
salary with studio officials. It was unlike her but it was
actually the best move Constance would ever make.

While Adolph Zukor was still counting box-office re-
ceipts from *Sullivan's Travels,* Paramount began readying
This Gun for Hire for release. The studio's advertising department launched a rather deceptive campaign. It included posters and publicity stills featuring Alan and

Veronica in several romantic poses, even though they never came within kissing distance during the film (except for the finale where Ladd dies in Veronica's arms).

Paramount's promotional experts knew what they were doing. *This Gun for Hire* opened on May 13, 1942, at the New York Criterion theatre. Produced at a cost of $500,000, the film went on to gross $12 million and to catapult Ladd straight to the top of Hollywood's list of leading men.

In this eighty-minute adventure yarn, Ladd plays the role of a hired gunman named the Raven, out to avenge a man who has double-crossed him. As the tough-as-nails nightclub siren, Ellen Graham, Veronica falls in love with a Los Angeles policeman (Robert Preston) who is assigned to capture Ladd. Hot on the Raven's trail, Preston heroically cracks the caper when he guns Ladd down, winning Veronica in the end. Paced by Frank Tuttle's air-tight direction, *This Gun for Hire* sparkles as top-notch entertainment and appeals to filmgoers of all ages. Al Maltz and W. R. Burnett also deserve credit for their fine screenplay adaptation of this rugged novel.

Critics believed the film offered a more realistic, if not equally farfetched, change of pace that projected "an icy magnetism between Veronica and Ladd." *Variety* commented on Ladd's death scene in Veronica's arms: "Better men have died with their heads in less pleasant places." *Life* magazine enthused: "Veronica, the paradox, can calm the fevered brow of a sick man with one stroke and with another can produce a fever in a well man." Leo Mishkin of the *Morning Telegraph* said it best, however, when he wrote: "You will probably be surprised to learn that in addition to being something to look at, Miss Lake is also emerging as a very fine actress, which is something entirely different these days."

But Veronica remained indifferent, and considered the film a comedown from her success in *Sullivan's Travels*. Now, she was back to wearing low-cut gowns, acting sexy, and creating an image of, as she put it, "everyman's mistress." But the studio couldn't have been more pleased with the results.

Smelling another chance to cash in on Veronica's growing popularity, Paramount's big three immediately paired Veronica with Alan Ladd in a remake of the Dashiell Hammett thriller, *The Glass Key*. In the Ladd–Lake version, Brian Donlevy was signed to appear as the tough political boss, and the cast included William Bendix, Bonita Granville, and Richard Denning. Veteran Frank Tuttle, who had directed Ladd and Lake in their first collaboration, was sidestepped in favor of newcomer Stuart Heisler.

According to Teet Carle, actress Patricia Morrison had originally been chosen over Lake but her tenure was short-lived. Filming with Morrison lasted only one day before she was suddenly let go from the picture. Evidently, Ladd felt ill-at-ease with Morrison's height, and his wife Sue Carol asked for her dismissal.

Carle remembers what led up to Morrison's removal, and Veronica's attempts to comfort the actress:

It was a good thing that Sue Ladd and Veronica got along so well. Alan was such a short person, that all his life he was haunted by tall people. He used to always say, 'Why do they constantly cast these secondary leads as tall young men? I can't help it if I'm this short.' After he made *This Gun for Hire*, Alan was cast in *The Glass Key*, but they put Patricia Morrison in it with him. They started the picture with Morrison and she was thrilled to be with Alan. They had one day of work as she loomed over him, so that was it. She was dropped from the picture. Now, they brought in Veronica. They called her and told her to come in for fittings because she was going to replace Morrison. But Veronica went afterward, not even calling ahead of time, to see Morrison and comfort her since the girl was brokenhearted. She said to her, 'You can't help it that you're tall, and neither can I that I am short. Just because you have a star shorter than you is not your fault.' Veronica's thoughtful remark bucked up Patricia, but she was never the same afterwards.

Surely Veronica bemoaned the means in which she was substituted for Morrison, but she probably welcomed the opportunity to work with Alan again since they made a good team. In this, her second film with Ladd, Veronica began noticing more clearly how Alan could "be cool, placid, all-observing and knowing, or just plain nasty." She admitted there were times when each of them thought of "shedding our individual shells and joining forces in a closer and perhaps more normal relationship," but nothing ever happened. Veronica and Alan would occasionally sit down and swap favorite stories, but they had less to do with each other than most other acting teams.

Veronica exhibited the same coolness and stony manner on the set, as she had in *This Gun for Hire.* When asked to discuss her histrionic abilities on the screen, Veronica answered, "I don't *think* I'm outstanding, in fact, I don't believe it is necessary to being a star. The audience doesn't want that, they don't want the best acting on the screen. What they want is personality, something new, something different."

Veronica would have made a good politician. She avoided the reporter's question completely, offering an entirely different answer. She must have been going through much pain at being separated from John, but she was unwilling to discuss it. Veronica was still upset over her salary, but not enough to march in and complain to the studio hierarchy. Every time she got angry at being exploited, she remembered the security her position provided and decided it would be foolish to jeopardize it.

Veronica was also angry at her mother. This time, Constance was meddling with an incident involving William Bendix, Veronica's co-star, and his wife, Tess. Veronica apparently adored Bendix, and they developed what she called "a purely platonic relationship." She made one mistake, though: she told her mother about it over the phone, and Constance went into action.

The day after Veronica's call, Constance met privately with Tess Bendix to warn her that Veronica was "trying to steal your Bill." It was one of the first times she had acted out of instinct for her daughter's sake, meaning no harm, however. But the situation turned into dynamite. Veronica had to soothe an unpleasant Tess Bendix, as well as mend the ways of her interfering mother. Afterward, Veronica stopped speaking to Constance. If the phone rang and it was her mother on the line, she would hang up without saying "hello." If she met Constance at the supermarket, she would mysteriously vanish. For the second time in her life, Veronica turned into a fugitive, running from her problems rather than facing them.

The Glass Key wasn't without its own mishaps. There was one incident in particular that preyed on Veronica's mind for the rest of her life. Brian Donlevy was the chief recipient. Donlevy had worked with Veronica before in *I Wanted Wings,* so he was well-aware of her explosive reputation on the set. What he didn't know but certainly found out was that she also possessed Herculean strength for her tiny size. For some reason, Donlevy never liked Veronica and made it known on several occasions with such hostile comments as, "Get out of my way, you little bitch." Veronica never discussed these verbal outbursts with him, but mulled privately on how to deal with Donlevy's abuse.

Somehow she planned to awaken Donlevy to that fact one morning following a coffee break. With the first scene ready to roll, Veronica strutted up on the set wearing a satin gown, her angelic hair flowing majestically over one eye. The scene called for her to punch Donlevy right in the jaw, missing him in the actual take, of course. Donlevy was a stocky man: he stood five feet eight inches tall, and weighed over two hundred pounds. Veronica, again, stood only five feet one inch and weighed approximately ninety-eight pounds. Director Stuart Heisler carefully instructed both actors on how to play the scene before ordering "Action!" Veronica froze as the cameras began running, afraid to carry out her plan. Finally letting loose, she put every ounce of energy behind her punch, striking Donlevy squarely on the jaw and staggering him. Dazed, Donlevy stared at Veronica, completely granite-faced, his mouth gaping open, with absolutely no movement in his body.

Snapping out of his stupor, Donlevy caught himself from falling and began seething when he focused on Veronica, saying, "What's your problem, little lady. Don't you know how to hit somebody?"

Playing dumb, Veronica said, "I don't know what you're talking about."

From that day forth, Veronica was clearly on Donlevy's "enemy list," his sore jaw serving as a reminder of Veronica's unpredictable and stormy personality.

Wrapping up production on *The Glass Key,* Veronica returned to Seattle to attend to a very personal matter: her marriage. For the second time in as many months, John vehemently demanded that she quit show business altogether. But Veronica knew only one way to handle the situation. She brooded and sulked daily, drowning her emotions in vodka, hoping the dilemma would somehow be resolved.

John had hoped that his status in the army would change things, that he would receive just as much attention as his wife. But instead, at social gatherings, John was still greeted by the classic, "Good evening Miss Lake . . . uh . . . Mr. Lake." Detlie had also become insanely jealous over the attention Veronica received from her fans. Fan letters only compounded this delicate situation, as they invariably asked about "Mister Lake." By now, Veronica was receiving over one thousand letters a week. She answered one out of every five letters personally. She tried appeasing her husband by signing each letter, "Mrs. John Detlie," but that didn't seem to satisfy his ego.

Veronica did manage to reconcile with John, spending more time with him to iron out these problems. Paramount had no new properties waiting for her at the moment, so she took a short hiatus to stay with John at the base, helping him design camouflage schemes for military installments and attending military social functions.

While her personal troubles began receding, Veronica's career kept skyrocketing. *The Glass Key* debuted in theaters nationwide on October 15, 1942. Veronica evoked a higher degree of coolness in her portrayal of Janet Henry, the vacillating, chic daughter of gubernatorial candidate Moroni Olsen. Thousands of fans lined up in front of the box office to catch their second glimpse of the Ladd–Lake combo, this time hoping for a little more romance than in their team debut.

Fans were not disappointed as Ladd and Veronica blended the right combination of ingredients, making this their second critical triumph in as many tries.

Critics agreed that *The Glass Key* chalked up another stunning performance for the young actress. Reflective of the public's adulation, James Corby of the *Brooklyn Daily Eagle* remarked: "What makes Veronica Lake such a good actress is the equipment she can bring to bear on a task in hand. Even without her voice and without her sense of timing in speech action, and without her ability to cast a spell over her audience with sheer modernity, Miss Lake would undoubtedly pass for a good actress, just by making her appearance in a scene. A girl with her surplus of charms is bound to get herself across anyway—but Veronica Lake is a fine actress as well."

Veronica's performance also captured the attention of her parents; Anthony and Constance had thirteen red roses delivered to her home. The bouquet was surely sentimental and softened Veronica's hard-nosed stance toward her mother. According to Constance, the thirteen roses symbolized a show of gratitude and love that her husband, Anthony, had started during Veronica's first year in show business. As she recalls: "My husband started it, for no reason really, other than that he idolized her. We always sent her on either her birthday or after a new picture thirteen red roses and thirteen new pennies. It was our way of congratulating her, but it also stemmed from that fact that Anthony just adored her."

The Glass Key rolled up some very impressive box-office numbers and concurrently pointed up another aspect of Veronica's appeal: her photogenic qualities.

Teet Carle believes that Lake's photogenic essence was unmatched by any actress in Hollywood. As he says: "Veronica was so photogenic with that velvety skinned cherubic face that photographers worked at ease and art editors on publications printed her photo by the hundreds. The creamy skin and spun golden hair made her head glitter. Her body needed no shadows or angling to hide unwanted bulges.

Carle also points out that "Veronica was really a plain

person without that makeup. When she went to Wally Westmore's [Paramount's makeup artist] and had makeup put on and her hair set, she always came out breathtaking. Just like an angel. You'd look at her in complete awe."

Julie Gibson, who also worked on the same lot with Veronica, saw Lake's overriding quality as having no limit on her sex appeal. In an interview, Gibson said that "Veronica was tiny but very sexy. There's no size limit on sex. I would say she was, what you'd call, a very delicate sexy. She came in a small package, but the sex was very much there. She had a very feline quality. There was also something sensuous and sultry about her, because she was catlike."

Veronica's feline sex appeal really showed to good advantage in Rene Clair's comedy *I Married a Witch,* her third film of 1942, co-starring Frederic March, Robert Benchley, Cecil Kellaway, and the young Susan Hayward. The film was produced by Preston Sturges at Paramount, and sold to United Artists as part of a package-distributing deal, but for Lake, landing the part hadn't been easy.

Veronica wanted the part of the witch; comedy was the escape she had been looking for, but Clair wasn't enthusiastic about having her in the film, saying that she was at her best playing "movie heavies," (such as in *This Gun for Hire*), and that comedy wasn't her style.

Veronica was very persistent, however. As her cousin Helene Nielsen relates: "When Veronica wanted a part, she really set her mind on getting that part. When it was given to someone else, though, she couldn't accept it."

Clair remained steadfast with his original veto, until Lake enlisted the support of her good friend Preston Sturges, who lobbied on her behalf. Sturges informed Clair that Veronica had very capably played a comic role in *Sullivan's Travels* and that comedy was like second nature to her. Preston claimed that he couldn't think of anyone more qualified for the role of Jennifer, the fair witch. Sturges' effective presentation sold Clair on switching his position, and Veronica was in.

During the second week of filming, Clair saw the first batch of rushes and afterward walked over to Veronica to apologize. He said, "I'm here to apologize, Ronni. Preston was right. You are one hell of a good comedienne. I'm sorry." Veronica accepted his apology, kissing him on the cheek in appreciation. Afterward, Clair and Veronica developed a very friendly relationship, which would endure after the picture was finished.

Veronica wished she could have said the same for her assertive co-star, Frederic March, surely the most despicable character she had ever worked with, (although Brian Donlevy also got a few votes). Teet Carle remembers that March had established himself as quite a womanizer, and Veronica was constantly on guard. As Carle recalls: "Frederic March had worked with many beautiful actresses, and found Veronica every bit as breathtaking. Well, she used to rail into him about being a horny old guy, since he tried making advances on her and the other women working in the film. He had a reputation for being on the make all the time."

March's flirtatious manner didn't set well with Veronica, creating an ongoing feud between them on the set. As the shooting went on, her intense dislike for him became more evident and the innate antagonism between the pair deepened. Veronica had heard that March had called her "a brainless little blond sexpot, void of any acting ability." Veronica had been a defiant child and she was a vengeful adult.

Her first plot to get even came when Veronica had a forty-pound weight sewn into her dress, so that when March had to lift her up for one scene, he could barely budge her. Veronica rigged the weight under her dress with the aid of the head cameraman. Naturally, March never thought he would have any problems picking up tiny Veronica. March grunted and groaned as he "valiantly carried out the script's directions and carried me off into the distance." Later, he commented to Lake on how much such a tiny woman like her weighed. She shrugged and supposedly remarked, "Big bones!"

Veronica's second chance at vengeance also occurred during the second week of filming. This time, during one scene, she was supposed to be rocking in a chair when a picture frame falls off the wall, rendering her unconscious. During the shot, March walks in and tries talking to Veronica, completely unaware that she's been knocked out. As March stood directly over her in the chair, she very carefully thrust her foot into his groin repeatedly. Actor that he was, Frederic never showed the slightest grimace of pain on his face until he finished the scene—shot from the waist up—at which time, Veronica smiled devilishly and March chased her off the set.

Director Rene Clair kept his distance from these two, rarely stepping in to mediate. Mischief-maker though she was, Veronica also knew enough to quit while she was ahead.

If Veronica's shenanigans didn't hamper production, her constant tardiness did. The studio frowned upon any actor showing up late, especially if it happened consistently. Lake had become an official member of that blacklisted group. In an interview, she remembered one such incident:

I had been called in for a portrait sitting with Freddie March for a certain day—and, well, time got away from me. Freddie, however, was on time. So was the photographer. There they sat and waited for me. Finally, they notified the front office and the front office called me. I tore down to the studio and found Freddie ready to slit my throat, for which I couldn't blame him, but at the moment it made me mad too. The crazy part of the whole affair was that we had to take love scenes, and, when I saw the finished results, I roared with laughter. Such pure loathing you've never seen on any two faces, particularly when they were lying so alluringly cheek-to-jowl. So I went to Freddie and apologized. He agreed to make the sitting over, and that time the results were slick.

After *I Married a Witch,* Veronica was cast in her fourth film of the year, a Paramount all-star feature called, *Star Spangled Rhythm.* Along with Lake, the film featured practically everyone from the Paramount lot: Alan Ladd, Bing Crosby, Bob Hope, Fred MacMurray, Ray Milland, Franchot Tone, Mary Martin, Dick Powell, William Bendix, Susan Hayward, Eddie Bracken, and Eddie "Rochester" Anderson, among others. The film also marked Betty Hutton's screen debut.

Veronica appeared in a gimmicky song number, "A Sweater, a Sarong, and a Peekaboo Bang," in which she, Paulette Goddard, and Dorothy Lamour lampooned their screen trademarks. Martha Mears was brought in to dub Veronica's singing voice—and for good reason. Lake's singing broke the eardrums of many actors waiting in the wings, including Bob Hope and Bing Crosby. As Veronica once remembered: "Bob Hope and Bing Crosby watched us do the song and I remember as I walked back to my dressing room, Hope stopped me and said, 'Hey, Veronica, you saving your money?' I said, 'Why, Bob?' He said, 'With a voice like *that,* you'll need it.' He was right. I could never sing."

Despite her lack of vocal talent, Veronica clearly possessed the ability to help the government's war bond program. Over the next year, beginning with her first tour in August 1942, she would sell over $12 million in bonds. Paramount's press agents had a field day with these figures. They estimated that based on one tour where she sold ten locks of hair for $186,000, if she sold her entire head of hair (equaling 150,000 strands) at the same rate, Veronica would raise over $2.7 million for the bond program. That was certainly a press agent's dream all right—but Veronica had only one head of hair to spare.

John, however, was unsupportive of her involvement in the program, preferring to have her busy with the chores of being a housewife and mother. John argued in vain, however. Veronica made the tour, only to regret her decision later.

9

...

Love and War

VERONICA FOUND that selling war bonds was grueling and unpleasant work. She lived out of a suitcase for nearly two months, never having time to herself, but handled the grueling assignment like a real pro. Her first stop on the tour was Fort Lewis to headline an open-house bond rally to which the public was invited. Veronica was the program's special guest, and the afternoon of the rally she sat on the reviewing stand alongside members of the army's top brass. Among the men resplendent in military green was John, who first refused to join the ceremonies but finally did so under orders from the ranking general.

John was clearly uncomfortable with Veronica's being put on display, and she knew he was upset. There had been no welcoming smile—no pride that she was the star attraction and that probably every man there envied him. She noticed that John seemed humiliated; he bowed his head constantly and seemed ashamed about what was going on around him. Nobody else knew why, but she did. Veronica had been uneasy about making this appearance. In fact, she had thought about faking an illness, but a team of army escorts had arrived before she could pull such a stunt.

Fort Lewis's four-star general got the ceremonies rolling when he introduced Veronica as "the great motion-picture star, Veronica Lake." As the throng cheered enthusiastically, Veronica rose to the rostrum and spoke eloquently about the war-bond program. She urged her countrymen to support America by "buying bonds, lots of bonds," to help in its military buildup to overthrow Hitler's powerful regime. It was only after she concluded her speech, to deafening applause, that the general realized he had overlooked John in the proceedings. Detlie's belated introduction to the crowd was acknowledged by scattered cheers—but they were not nearly as enthusiastic as those Veronica had received moments earlier. Most of the crowd, in fact, had exited the grounds, leaving only a few patriotic supporters to greet John warmly.

Veronica left the next morning on a five-week tour that would take her through the southern and eastern states, ending in New York. John was going to miss her, but at the same time, he was still angry over her priorities. Once more, he tried urging her to resign from the tour—to stay with him and raise Elaine in a proper family environment. But Veronica boldly explained, "My country has called me, just like it called you to duty. That comes above my marriage or my career." It is not possible to guess at her real motives. She did love John and she was patriotic, but she was also frightened of family responsibilities.

John gave up fighting on the home front. Either she returned home after this tour under his conditions, or it was time to dissolve their marriage once and for all. The latter would be a final desperate admission that he and Veronica were finished—and John wasn't desperate . . . yet.

Veronica considered the christening of a navy aircraft carrier at a local shipyard in Jacksonville, Florida, the biggest thrill of her bond tour. She had never been given such an honor before and she accepted it with great trepidation. When it came to breaking the bottle of champagne correctly, she was afraid that she wouldn't have enough sock. But she did, and with such force, in fact, that she splattered everybody standing near her.

She also made her equal share of enemies along the way. In Boston, where she was the scheduled guest speaker for a nighttime rally, Veronica arrived almost an hour late for reasons that have never been explained. She may have been drinking; she may just have been the victim of her own disregard for time. Pulling the unexpected, which was becoming her trademark, Veronica proceeded to berate the assembled crowd for not respecting her dignity as a star. She gained no friends that evening with either the press or her public.

But the highlight of Veronica's tour had yet to come. Her last stop was New York City. This time her visit took on a more sentimental nature as she revisited the Statue of Liberty, Times Square lit up in all its glory, and Yankee Stadium. The city was electrifying, the people enthusiastic, and her reception the warmest of any stop on the tour.

Veronica climaxed her thirty-city tour with a huge rally at Madison Square Garden. Over five thousand people jammed the arena to hear her upbeat speech on "crushing the Nazis" and "helping our brave soldiers overseas." Many were startled by the fact that her voice, which was soft in ordinary conversations, boomed out strong and loud from the platform. Stopping periodically during her speech, the audience automatically roared and cheered her on. Afterward, Veronica was led out of the arena to shake hands with an entourage of admirers. One thing Veronica rarely forgot were her fans. She usually found time to sign autographs and exchange pleasantries.

That doesn't mean that some fans didn't present problems. Because of her sexy image, Teet Carle remembers that many of her fans wanted to touch more than her hand. "A woman by the name of Dale Rooks went with Veronica. I remember she said it was the hardest job she ever had. Veronica was a real sexpot and everywhere she went she insisted on having a stateroom, or bedroom, where she could lock herself in. Dale said half of her job was keeping the sailors, soldiers, and blue-collar workers from knocking on her door. All of them wanted to get in and be with Veronica."

According to Veronica's mother, her daughter sometimes thought less of these flocks of followers than was publicly known. "She would receive many nice things from fans during her tours, but no matter what people did for her or gave her, she would rarely thank them either personally or with a note. I would get so embarrassed sometimes that I would send these fans thank you notes and sign her name."

Her occasional oversight of her fans' tokens of admiration might have been due to the fact that she never really cared much for all the adulation. As Helene Nielsen explains: "She enjoyed it to a certain degree, but when it was enough, she wanted to be secluded, because she was so wound up emotionally."

Following the last leg of her cross-country journey, Veronica's biggest challenge still lay ahead. She now had to face John. She felt his ultimatum was unfair, that she could be both housewife and actress if he would only be reasonable. Veronica might very well be called one of American's earliest examples of a liberated woman; or she might only have been a selfish one. She wanted everything a man had, only more. With her career peaking, she once said, "My ego got in the way."

Veronica returned home on October 5, 1942. The minute she walked inside the door, John said, "Hello," then in the same breath, "So, Ronni, I need an answer. Are you going to stop this foolishness and give up your career for the sake of Elaine and me?"

She countered with another question of her own: "Is that fair, John? I think I can do both."

John was silent. He was never very assertive in his arguments with Veronica.

As he turned and left the room, Veronica remained stubbornly mute. She would have her way . . . not his. She was almost ready to boot John out of her life like an old shoe and start having fun with men who were more her type —feisty yet fun-loving. But they stuck it out a while longer— John hoping that Veronica would change; Veronica hoping wistfully that it would all somehow work out.

Around this time, Veronica's drinking habits became more pronounced. She kept her drinking bouts reserved to the privacy of her own home, where she sat hopelessly in front of a glass of Scotch or vodka, contemplating her future. She knew now that that future wouldn't be with John. Meanwhile, John paid little attention to her drinking, hoping that his silence would bring Veronica to her senses.

Eventually the subject of this discussion was dropped, but not forgotten. Winning for the moment, Veronica's will was next tested when Paramount assigned her to her first production for 1943, *So Proudly We Hail.*

Veronica was cast as Olivia D'Arcy, one of three nurses belonging to the fighting force of Bataan, who tries outdueling the enemy. Paulette Goddard and Claudette Colbert, both capable actresses in their own right, co-starred in the film as the two other nurses. The screenplay was based on true accounts of the surviving nurses from Bataan.

John was anything but satisfied over Veronica's latest acting opportunity. He operated under the rule of "all or nothing." Veronica's decision to meet him only halfway was not enough. She tried hiding her concern, but it was evident to some of her closest friends that trouble was brewing.

She did fool some stars, among them, Mary Treen, who co-starred and narrated *So Proudly We Hail.* Treen recalls that Veronica was very mysterious to everyone and that it was impossible to detect whether she was suffering. As she explains: "Veronica was in several scenes in the picture, but she had a certain reserved manner as though she knew all the answers. She was probably concerned over her most dramatic scene in the film."

According to others who knew her, it is doubtful she was more concerned about her performance than she was about her public image. She continued to make news. *So Proudly We Hail* would not only become a landmark film for her career but would also mark the first time since *Sullivan's Travels* that her shapely hairdo was confined under a cap. Newspaper syndicates as well as newsreel producers immediately picked up on this story. One wire service reported that "Veronica Lake's new up-do hairdress, which abandons her famous peekaboo bang as a Bataan nurse in *So Proudly We Hail,* has become a newsreel subject. Paramount News, on assignment from New York, following news that Veronica is cooperating with the War Production Board in inducing women war workers to avoid long, loose hairstyles, photographed the blond star dressing her 27-inch hair on top of her head."

Legend has it that Veronica's hairstyle had become so imitated, that the War Production Board requested that she refrain from wearing her hair down for the duration of the war. Evidently, many female war workers sporting Lake coiffures were getting their tresses caught in the machinery. Thus, Veronica supposedly patriotically complied with the War Production Board's request. Some years later, believing the story herself, she wrote that this issue became a matter of "congressional record."

The story wasn't true. Actually, it was just another publicity stunt, according to Teet Carle. "We did that. And we got big play out of her getting her hair cut. It sounded good and it was just one of our publicity dreams. In those days, newspapers and magazines had so many columns coming out daily that they all wanted material. So, when there was never enough, we had to start fabricating it. As I say today, we were experts at deceit and dishonesty."

Even though the story was believed to be true at the time, Veronica was never overly concerned about how her fans were going to react to her new hairstyle. She was also unconcerned over the size of her role. It was one of the shortest performances in her career up to that point, as Teet Carle remembers: "Veronica must have liked the role because, even going back to *I Wanted Wings,* the audience remembered her for the death scene in the end. In this film, she would also be remembered for her grapple with death."

Veronica enjoyed her small but complete portrayal. As she once recalled in an interview: "Let me make it clear that I don't worry over the size of my roles. Certainly, the part I played in *So Proudly We Hail* was a little more than a bit. It was a good part and that's what matters."

The scene happens during the last thirty minutes of the film in which Veronica, with a grenade snug in her bosom, surrenders to the Japanese. Just as she reaches the crowd of awaiting Japanese soldiers, the grenade that she had triggered explodes and kills her and the enemy instantly. It is a scene that vividly deserves recognition and also convincingly portrays the kind of heroism that often made headlines during the battle of Bataan.

What also mattered to Paramount's executives were stories circulating on Veronica's private and personal life. Word was out that she had suddenly become sexually assertive with "just about every technician at the studio," including a prominent producer, who shall remain nameless. According to doctors, schizophrenics often exhibit sexual behaviors that are opposite of the principles and morals on which they were raised.

Veronica's first sexual encounter with the unnamed Paramount producer happened one night while she was making the rounds at local bars. Every night, she would hop in the car and drive to the slummy part of Los Angeles, near Central Avenue, to drink as much as she could. Having a drink in her hand seemed the only reasonable thing in her world. Even though earlier in her life she preferred drinking alone, by now she enjoyed socializing with others who had troubles like her own. Her romance with the producer followed one of her drunken binges, as Constance Marinos remembers:

> She started hanging around low-grade people, drunks, bums, you name it. In fact, for a while she lived down in the bowery of Los Angeles and would be seen drinking every night at many clubs in the area, including The Merry-Go-Round, which was owned by Alice Faye's brother. As far as I was concerned, she became a non-person at this point. She'd go to the studio stoned drunk the next day, and they'd have to

send her home. It was when she was in one of those drunken stupors that she started her romance with this producer.

When Veronica wasn't partying at nightclubs, she carried on at her Mandeville Canyon home. It became a weekly hangout for people she'd made friends with on the strip, with Veronica providing free booze and sex.

John Engstead, an art supervisor at Paramount at the time, recalls that news of Veronica's affairs could be heard through the grapevines daily. "Veronica was a nice enough lady burdened with more bosoms than brains. I remember she was also going at the time with a nice looking prop man, whose name escapes me. Besides his looks, this young man, so the scuttlebutt went, had a penis in proportion to Veronica's bosoms."

Following her alcoholic and sexual excesses, Veronica's mother reports that her house was usually left a shambles, with no trace of food other than empty liquor bottles strewn all over. "It was horrible. She was playing around and had everybody running around her house. I went there one day and there was a note from someone who had stayed over. It said, 'Thanks, jerk, for the use of the hall.' There were also empty liquor bottles lying all over the place. It was like something you'd see in one of Hitchcock's movies. The beds were never made, and it was as if she didn't care anymore. She even started turning nasty with people at the studio. So when they saw her coming down the walk at Paramount, they'd say, 'Here comes that bitch, Veronica Lake.' I don't believe she knew what she was doing."

John Engstead also recounted that Veronica's kitchen resembled something out of the classic nursery rhyme, "Old Mother Hubbard." Recalling one incident, he says:

One night I left Paramount with Lindsay Durand, one of Paramount's publicists, who said that Veronica wanted us over for dinner at her house. So it was arranged and Lindsay and I drove to her house in Mandeville Canyon. She had her friend the prop man over that night too. But when we got there, Lindsay noticed there wasn't a maid, no cook, no one to meet us. The kid, Elaine, was in bed, and nothing was said about eating after we were there. So about nine o'clock, Lindsay finally said something about food and we all went into the kitchen. There was no preparation, and no food in the house. So the prop man and I drove to a market in Santa Monica, and bought bacon, eggs, bread, and butter, and returned to have this for dinner. Afterward, Lindsay and I could never understand this.

Veronica's cupboards were bare, in part, due to her generosity with her needy friends. If one of them needed a thousand dollars for an operation, she would slap the money in that person's hands without asking any questions. Often times, the money slipped out of her hands as fast as she earned it. She would always spend her money on others, but when it came to Elaine, or as later years would prove, her other children, that was an entirely different story. She never viewed them as her responsibility, and was not concerned with taking care of them—on any level. Caretakers were good enough. But although she was a horrible mother, it should not be forgotten that she could not take care of herself.

She also spent her money foolishly in nightclubs and bars. Once, when she was drinking in the Beverly Hills Hotel Polo Room, Veronica paid not only for her drinks but for everybody else in the house.

Veronica had other distorted values. Forgetting the

principles the Catholic Church taught, Constance recalls what her daughter would tell her—not once, but many times. "In my own living room, she'd stand there and call me 'a goddamn Catholic.' The trouble with me was that I was supposed to have sex with other men. She said that to me. My husband said if she ever told him that, he'd shove her teeth down her neck. I felt the best thing wasn't to say anything. I just couldn't reason with her anymore."

In an attempt to bring Veronica out of her personal quagmire, Mrs. Keane also tried taking her daughter to dinner at some of the most expensive restaurants in town, including Romanoff's. She hoped that by reminding Veronica of what her life used to be like she might be able to bring her back to reality. But that attempt to help the troubled star also failed. "One time, we took her to a very elegant restaurant nearby and it cost us five hundred dollars for the dinner. I wanted to show her the way she was brought up, and the way she used to live. But it didn't work. She was very degraded mentally."

On other occasions, Veronica would take these dining opportunities to accuse her mother repeatedly for not giving her a happy childhood. These incidents were explained by doctors as "persecutory delusions," in which the patient blames others for her suffering. As Mrs. Keane tells it: "I gave her everything she wanted as a child. We took her to so many places that when people would look at our photo albums, they thought we were millionaires. But whenever we went out to the movies or dinner, it never failed. Out of the clear blue sky, she'd say, 'I never had a happy childhood.' I'd say, 'I wished I'd had one.' Then, she'd say, 'The kids didn't come in the house to see me, they came to see you, because anything I could do, you could do better.' My husband used to tell me she was just jealous, but I never thought of it that way."

Although Veronica's reputation around the studio had

worsened, she did agree to appear by telephone on a segment of *We the People,* a popular weekly human-interest radio program. The CBS show featured interviews with civilians who had survived unusual experiences and, at times, various Hollywood celebrities stood in front of the microphone to recall their own hair-raising tales.

The week Veronica was on the show, it was broadcast from the University of Pennsylvania, and during the program the host recruited a student from the audience to participate in a special segment called "Talk to Your Favorite Celebrity." The student's selection was, of course, Veronica; she was very popular with young college men.

The ensuing phone conversation, which was patched through to Veronica's Mandeville Canyon home, only further illustrated her changing attitude about herself. Teet Carle, who drove to Lake's home to set up the phone conversation, remembers that incident:

> I went out to see her at eleven in the morning on that day of the broadcast. When I got there, she was all alone in the house and she had a cold. Her hair was up in a silly knot, and she wore one of her husband's sweatshirts, the gaudiest pants you've ever seen, and some sagging stockings. To top it off, she also had these ugly bedroom slippers on her feet, and was using the carpet sweeper as I was setting up the phone conversation. She certainly didn't look like the beautiful, charming sexpot, but I was accustomed to that. Finally, when the call came through, I told her to shut off the sweeper and handed her the phone. She told this student on the other end, "Oh, you shouldn't be awed by me. Why I'm no different than any of the co-eds you have on campus." I got up laughing and went into the next room, thinking, "My God, there isn't a co-ed anywhere who looks as terrible as she does right now." If only that guy could have seen what

she looked like, he would have probably preferred any co-ed over her.

Although Paramount was constantly beset by the conflict between the often publicized details of Veronica's private life troubling her public image, Adolph Zukor remained unusually calm in the midst of this crisis: he knew that Veronica was still a big moneymaker for the studio. They had too big an investment in her to back down so quickly. They would try to milk her dry first. With one film scheduled for October release, *I Married a Witch,* Veronica's box-office domination looked as strong as ever. Given its premiere on October 30, 1942, the film broke many house records in theaters across the country, and once again clearly established Veronica's abilities as a comedienne. Filmgoers stomped their feet with laughter while watching Veronica, playing a Salem witch, outmaneuver Susan Hayward (Frederic March's fiancee in the film) with her bewitching powers.

Critics didn't seem to mind either, as her sensual and comic prowess combined for a performance that they generally praised as being both artistic and entertaining. Bosley Crowthers of *The New York Times* wrote: "The strange and beautiful illusion that Veronica Lake is completely unreal is being quite charmingly nourished in Rene Clair's new film, *I Married a Witch.* You recall that Miss Lake was first manifest on the screen as an ambulating hank of hair from behind which emerged dulcet noises and a calorific glow. If you have been of the faction wondering what constitutes the allure of Veronica Lake, this picture may solve your dilemma. You never saw a more hexy display from any witch."

With her value rising and maturing faster than savings bonds, Paramount knew that they would have to contend with a raise in salary sooner or later. Her earnings of $750 a week were ludicrous compared to the salaries of other stars of her stature. Bob Hope and Bing Crosby were taking home $5,000 a week, including dividends on hundreds of shares of stock in the company. And Paramount's sarong girl, Dorothy Lamour, wasn't far behind.

Veronica threatened to walk out if her salary weren't increased, but Paramount countered with threats to either cancel her contract, or put her on suspension, if she dared. Child that she was, her defiance soon waned and she went back to the business of making movies.

Her next film, *So Proudly We Hail,* started production on November 28, 1942, and temporarily disbanded production just before the Christmas holidays. At home for Christmas, with the residual effects of her feud with John still clouding the holiday, Veronica received something to cheer about. *Life* magazine had voted her the "Top Female Box Office Attraction of 1942." Her rise to the top seemed even more unprecedented when an army poll also rated her "the most popular actress of the year." Two marines in the South Pacific stationed on an unchartered volcanic island, both captivated by this voluptuous star, named the tiny piece of land "Veronica Island."

When filming resumed three weeks later, however, Veronica was almost lost to Paramount indefinitely. She started developing excruciating stomach pains followed by nausea. This discomfort recurred in the middle of the night, and became more severe in the wee hours of the morning. On January 10, 1943, she was rushed to Good Samaritan Hospital for a routine examination. There Dr. Arnold Stevens found that her white-cell count was low, indicating the possibility of venereal disease.

Reporting his findings, Stevens tentatively asked, "Have you been having intercourse, Miss Lake?"

Veronica flatly denied the charge. "How could you even think such a thing possible? I haven't been sleeping with my husband, let alone someone else's."

"Sorry," Stevens told her, "but because of the lab findings I had to check out that possibility."

Veronica had probably been sleeping around, at least if there was any truth in the rumors about her wild parties and her involvement with the well-endowed prop man and the producer, who was married. It later turned out that Veronica's appendix was at fault, and an appendectomy was scheduled that evening. John had received news of the operation and called his wife from Seattle. Veronica assured him she was going to be all right and that the doctors expected she'd be returning to work in about a week.

Veronica was back on the Paramount lot in four days. She appeared to have regained her stamina, but according to *So Proudly We Hail* co-star Ann Doran, Lake took advantage of her weakened condition and held up production for sympathy:

> Veronica came back really before she should have. I recall it was four days after the operation. They hadn't even taken the stitches out yet. And boy did she play up the fact that, "I'm the invalid." She embraced it, and she used it. I must say that Mark Sandrich saw right through her; he didn't succumb to it. But she used the hairdresser and wardrobe woman or anybody close by, regardless of position, to help her around the set. The person I felt sorry for the most was the assistant director. She made his life hell. It was his business along with the second assistant director to get everybody there when they were ready to shoot. But, half the time, they waited on Veronica. If she had to make a slight costume change, she wouldn't go to her dressing room on the set, but to her dressing room across

the lot! The assistant director would have to get her, while the rest of us waited. At the time, they brought her over in a wheelchair, which I think was only right because of her condition. But the assistant director took the flak from Sandrich if she wasn't on the set.

But Veronica's bill of good health only held until after *So Proudly We Hail* completed production two weeks later. Several days later, the stomach pains began recurring. This time, Dr. Raymond McBurney, her family physician, examined Veronica more closely and informed her the next day, "You're pregnant, Miss Lake."

Veronica wasn't delighted over the news. How was she going to tell John? As expected, he took the news badly, knowing full well that the baby wasn't his.

"What have you been doing, sleeping around?" John asked, anger burning brightly in his eyes.

"Well . . ." Veronica paused to assemble her defense: "You should know better than to accuse me of that."

John was not convinced. Their marriage had been coming apart for a long time, and that one second of stammering told him the whole story. The baby's father was the producer, according to Constance, but he would later claim no responsibility for the child, leaving Veronica in hysterics. Meanwhile, every time John brought up the subject, Veronica flatly denied ever having an affair. Had she spoken up and been her most convincing, she might have remained Mrs. John Detlie a lot longer. Instead, it seemed as if she had simply given up on her life with John, that the marriage had reached its breaking point.

10

· · · ·

It's Too Late

VERONICA WAS BECOMING more despondent every day. With her second pregnancy, her drinking also accelerated and she continued to hang around downtown Los Angeles with the lowlife. What upset Veronica the most, however, was that she didn't want the responsibility of another child. Elaine was enough. More often than not, her drinking would result in sadistic acts. One such incident occurred several weeks after she discovered that she was pregnant.

Elaine was still living with Veronica at the Mandeville Canyon home. Both were preparing to rejoin John in Seattle, before Veronica was to report for her next film, *The Hour Before the Dawn.* The evening before her departure, Veronica returned home from the market and found that Elaine had been left unattended by the nursemaid. Elaine, now three years old, was playing in the house when her mother entered. Veronica, who had been drinking, stumbled over some furniture, before finding her way to her daughter. On being picked up, Elaine suddenly wet her diaper. As if in defiance of her motherhood, Veronica became enraged, and instead of changing the diaper, began to savagely beat her daughter. The nursemaid, who had gone into the kitchen to fetch Elaine's bottle, rushed into the living room to break up the incident, but Veronica shoved her aside. She wanted to teach her daughter a lesson. Elaine wailed in pain and incomprehension.

One of her next door neighbors, Mrs. McCloud, heard Elaine screaming and immediately called the police to report the beating. Meanwhile, Veronica's mother received a call from Rita Beery, informing her that she better drive down to the scene as quickly as possible.

Recalling the incident, Constance says today: "I got there before the police, and put Veronica, the nursemaid, and Elaine in the car and drove to the borderline of California to make sure that she was going to see John in Seattle. Since she didn't have a nickel, I gave her twenty-five dollars and sent her on her way, taking Elaine back with me to my house. Veronica did these things unconsciously, and she would always tell me later, 'Mommy, I don't understand why I am this way.' "

Police cars arrived at the scene moments later, but with no evidence of a beating apparent, the incident was passed off as nothing more than a crank call.

In explaining her daughter's unusual behavior toward Elaine, Mrs. Keane says, "She had Elaine, but as far as she was concerned she wasn't hers. This would be her same feeling with the other children, like they were somebody else's. She was never cut out to be a mother, that's for sure."

Once things cooled off, Veronica returned to Hollywood to begin filming her latest movie, *The Hour Before the Dawn,* based on W. Somerset Maughan's novel about wartime England. The film reunited Veronica with Frank Tuttle, who had directed her previously in *This Gun for Hire.* Co-stars included Franchot Tone, John Sutton, and Binnie Barnes, with location filming set in Phoenix, Arizona. Principal photography commenced on April 30, 1943.

Production of *The Hour Before the Dawn* brought to light for the first time the unusual relationship that was developing between Veronica and Wallace Beery's ex-wife, Rita, who had been one of her next-door neighbors when she had lived with her parents in Beverly Hills. Veronica and Rita became friends after Lake's relationship with her own mother began to falter. Rita was everything that her mother was not: undemanding and highly compassionate. Rita was a self-professed lesbian, who would later invite Veronica to live with her. It is known that they became quite close, but the exact nature of their relationship is unknown. Although Veronica's mother doesn't know "whether it is true," her schizophrenic condition may have provoked deviant sexual actions. It is known that Veronica requested that Rita join her on location to share living quarters with her, as Teet Carle explains: "This friendship existed to the point that Veronica invited Rita down with her when she did the picture. Veronica wanted Rita down there, in fact, she requested it. And Rita stuck very close to Veronica all the time."

According to Constance, Rita was like "a second mother figure" to Veronica. She consoled her over her problems, but at the same time used her. Beery would pose as "Mrs. Constance Keane" whenever she went out to deal with the local merchants. This annoyed Veronica's real mother, but she didn't know how to combat the problem and left well enough alone.

Teet Carle also noticed that Veronica had become even more rebellious at this point in her life. He recalled that she was disgruntled over filming conditions, over her dressing room, and over the long hours she was working. Nothing pleased her and she wanted a change . . . an immediate change, knowing only one way to have her needs granted. She would have an intimate talk with the producer, who also happened to be her lover. As Teet Carle recalls:

> With all the things that were happening to her, Veronica was always conniving and [she] wasn't subtle about it. The film's producer, who she was having an affair with, was coming down there and I remember Veronica saying that she was happy since he was coming to straighten things out. She said, "This is the greatest thing that's ever happened to me." I said, "Why's that, Veronica?" She said, "They're not giving me what I want. But so-and-so gets in on the plane at seven o' clock. So, by eight o'clock I'll have him in bed and by nine o'clock I will have anything I want."

Even though Veronica was several months pregnant, she didn't let her condition restrict her from having sex with her producer/lover, if it meant that she would get what she wanted. And the following day, he complied with her every wish.

Her actions might have been amoral, but, child that she was, Veronica carefully plotted to get what she wanted at any cost.

Back in Hollywood, Veronica was being seriously considered to portray the role of a native girl named Three Martini in Cecil B. DeMille's *Story of Dr. Wassell.* Word was also out that Veronica would be retiring from active studio duty once her second child was born, but she flatly denied both rumors. It would have been interesting, to say the least, if these two personalities had worked together because both were volatile individuals.

Then, on June 22, 1943, Paramount's flag-waving tribute to the brave nurses of Bataan, *So Proudly We Hail,* opened at Radio City Music Hall in New York. The film exceeded the studio's own expectations. Reviewers also became unresistingly patriotic, awarding the film their highest critical kudos. The *New York Daily Mirror* reported: "Veronica not only gives the finest performance of her youthful career, but steps out in front as one of the Hollywood greats."

Wrapping up integral filming for *The Hour Before the Dawn,* Veronica became increasingly moody, still resenting the fact that she was going to have a baby. The evening she finished filming *The Hour Before the Dawn,* Veronica was scheduled for a rehearsal on Groucho Marx's radio program, *Blue Ribbon Town.* In her haste to leave the studio on time, she supposedly tripped over a lighting cable that was stretched across the sound stage, triggering early labor. That was the story, at least, that both Veronica and newspapers reported at the time. But that wasn't what happened.

Teet Carle, who kept his distance from Veronica during her second pregnancy, remembers that it was common knowledge throughout the studio that Veronica didn't want the baby. The incident involving the lighting cable was a cover-up to protect Veronica's image. Instead, she had tried to abort the baby by causing a miscarriage:

> To show you how she would do some absolutely shocking things, when she was pregnant again, she didn't want the baby and tried having a miscarriage. In fact, she did this when she was over at Rita Beery's

house one evening. She became hysterical and climbed high up on a stool, screaming, "I don't want this baby, I don't want this baby. . . ." Rita tried telling her, "Come on, Veronica, you're playing with your life." She wouldn't listen . . . she jumped off the stool, landing on the edge of her heels. She went to great lengths to do what she believed, even if it would end in injury.

After her fall, Veronica felt a gush of fluid streaming inside her body. Hemorrhaging had started, and she was losing blood rapidly. She was immediately taken by ambulance to Good Samaritan Hospital where reports of her condition were filed daily. Veronica was admitted to the hospital on July 2, 1943.

If it had not been for her mother, however, she might have never made it. As Constance recalls:

> I came over and took her to the hospital. It was during an electrical blackout in the city and I didn't know where Rita Beery's house was. I heard an ambulance careening down Sunset Boulevard and tried driving abreast with the ambulance. I started honking and got the attention of one of the attendants, and he told me to follow them. When we got there, my husband refused to go in, so I went in by myself. In those days, it was only fifteen dollars for an ambulance. But neither Rita or Veronica had fifteen cents between them, so I had to go over and get a check from my husband to pay for the ambulance ride to the hospital. What I went through with her, you'd think I was on marijuana and was dreaming these things up.

What prompted Veronica to jump was the news that the producer's wife wouldn't give him a divorce. She wanted him to acknowledge that he was the father of their child, but it was impossible. Lake became hysterical—she had always been under the impression that he was going to marry her.

On her first day in the hospital, Dr. Raymond McBurney had her undergo prenatal observation to determine the extent of any damage to the baby. Tests proved inconclusive. McBurney was hoping to prevent the premature birth of the child, but nature had already taken its course.

Veronica was only in her sixth month of pregnancy. With her condition steadily declining, she was given periodic blood transfusions. She kept screaming for John and asking McBurney and the nurses to call him to be at her side. Near tears, she told McBurney, "Doc, I don't want this baby. I just don't. Please help me." McBurney called John, who informed the doctor that since the baby wasn't his, he wouldn't be coming.

Meanwhile, Veronica's mother was stationed outside her daughter's room. She brought a quilt and a pillow from home and slept in a chair during her vigil. When the news of Lake's hospitalization flashed through Paramount, nobody sent her so much as *one* rose.

Constance called Lindsay Durant at Paramount about having some flowers sent to Veronica's room. Durant tried organizing a flower fund, but as she told Constance, "I spoke to people about sending flowers but they said, 'That goddamn bitch, I wouldn't send her anything.' "

When Veronica learned that John wasn't coming, she sought compassion from another man, Dr. McGee, the assisting physician. She became sexually involved with McGee, asking him to marry her. As Constance recalls: "Veronica got involved with this Dr. McGee, and wanted him to leave his wife over her. When I heard about this, I went to consult her. I said, 'Connie, don't you know he's married?' She said to me, 'This is the twentieth century.' But this didn't last long either. McGee never left his wife because he started feeling guilty."

Mrs. Keane tried talking sense into John, trying to convince him that he was needed at the hospital. She advised him, since he wasn't a Catholic, to consult the army chaplain for advice if he wouldn't listen to her. John said, "I'll try to come if things let up." He didn't try hard enough.

Veronica gave birth on July 8 to a three-pound boy named William Anthony Detlie (he was named William after the producer). Despite around-the-clock observation, young William's condition turned critical on the second day. Doctors gave the premature infant blood transfusions but nothing helped as uremic poisoning set in. Seven days later, on July 15, 1943, William was pronounced dead at 10:10 A.M. As far as Veronica was concerned, her marriage to John also died.

It was easier to blame this entire mess on John than to accept her own role in it. Detlie arrived the next day to help with the funeral arrangements and the baby was cremated. Attending the services were John, Veronica, Constance and Anthony Keane, and Father McGovern, the pastor of Good Sheperd Catholic Church, a close friend of the Keanes. Unlike her days in the hospital, scores of flowers and wreaths were delivered to the mortuary to pay homage to young William.

Still weak from the operation, Veronica never spoke a word to John. She stared silently at the front of the mortuary's chapel, reviewing what had transpired. After the ceremonies ended, John rode back with Veronica, Constance, Anthony, and Father McGovern in a chauffeur-driven limousine. Separated from the driver by a glass partition, silence permeated the passenger cabin until John broke his own, saying, "I'm sorry, Veronica. I'm sorry . . ." His voice trailed off as he fought back the tears.

Choking back her own grief, Veronica sat helplessly, confused and lost, only able to blame John and not herself for what had happened. "It's too late, John. It's too late for apologies, you've done enough."

11

· · · ·

Going It Alone

WITH A DIVORCE IMMINENT, Veronica was still not out of the storm. Convalescing from the baby's birth in early August 1943, Veronica denied as "a lot of gossip," rumors that any rift had arisen in her marriage to the former MGM art director. As Lake told a *Los Angeles Times* reporter: "I have *never* had any idea of a separation or divorce." Her closest friends knew better, and two weeks later, on August 23, 1943, Veroncia made such gossip official only one month before their second wedding anniversary when she filed for divorce from John on the grounds of "irreconcilable differences." Veronica has said that the actions that ensued were "peaceful, but there was little communication" between her and her husband. Packing up her troubles in Seattle, Lake returned to her Mandeville Canyon home until divorce proceedings were over. When the pending divorce action was first publicly announced, Veronica told members of the press that "we have agreed after a long discussion of our problems to get a divorce . . . this is the only solution."

In the opinion of the newspaper editors, Veronica's divorce deserved full treatment because of the unusual circumstances that preceded the court proceedings. When Superior Court Judge Stanley Mosk presided over the case on October 5, 1943, newspaper reporters jammed the courtroom to hear the evidence. On the first day of the hearing, Lake appeared cheerful. She was wearing a tan trench coat, a muffler, and a plain tam o'shanter concealing her famous blond bang. Defense Attorney Morton Garbus acted on Lake's behalf.

In a voice so quiet it was barely audible, Veronica charged that John objected to her career, the travel that it involved, and said she was not "a fit mother" for their child. As she told the court: "He couldn't understand why I had to travel over the country instead of being with him. I was going through quite a lot. I had been quite ill on my bond tour, and then I went through surgery—and then my child —and with my husband, too, well it was just a little too much to take. He even objected to my friends so much that finally I had no friends at all. He'd telephone and insult me, then send me flowers."

To these accusations, even though none of them carried even one ounce of truth, John made no reply. Veronica was convincing, but supporting testimony from her corroborating witness and confidante, Rita Beery, sewed up the verdict in her favor. Thus, on December 8, 1943, Judge Mosk awarded final custody of Elaine to Veronica, proclaiming her to be "a fit mother," and set John's alimony payments at forty dollars a month. Detlie received visitation rights of up to three months a year with Elaine. Unfortunately, in the months ahead, Veronica proved that John had been right about her—she was irresponsible and an unfit mother. Throughout these bad times, Veronica would again try tugging at the heartstrings of her friends and fans for sympathy and support.

In the September 1943 edition of *Photoplay* magazine, Hedda Hopper penned an article entitled "Heartbreak for Veronica Lake" that reviewed the events leading up to her broken marriage with John. In the published article, Hopper asked Lake one last question at the conclusion of the interview. It was: "I suppose the minute you're divorced you'll remarry?"

Veronica flatly stated, "Well, I hope when I do that, I'll have a little bit more sense than I've had in the past."

Hopper ended the article with the following observation: "I said it would take something drastic to bring Veronica and John together again. Perhaps, that something has now happened in this tragedy that has come to them both. Out of heartbreak may come a measure of happiness."

Sounds good, doesn't it? *Photoplay* gave its readers a glimmer of hope, indicating that perhaps John and Veronica would reconcile and live happily ever after. Although that might be a Hollywood formula, the real conclusion to Hopper's article was deleted. In the original manuscript, the famous movie columnist asked Veronica one additional question after Lake's comment on marriage.

Hopper asked, "Why? Don't you like men?"

Veronica softly replied, "Yes, they're a necessary evil. I can't live without 'em. But they're all a lot of *bastards.*" Obviously, *Photoplay*'s editors believed fans were not prepared for such a remark. In time, however, fans and the public would discover what made Veronica really tick.

Veronica was now free and celebrated with a bottle of booze. Her drinking continued to control her. It was her only escape. Although she often preferred solitary drinking, during this time Veronica became a regular on Hollywood's social circuit. In an interview, she admitted how much she was enjoying life as a single: "Sure. I've gone out dancing since I've been separated. It seems to me a girl who is twenty-one and has worked hard all day is entitled to a bit of finding onself and dancing now and again. But the very fact I had a half a dozen different dates shows that I wasn't serious about any of them."

Veronica was dating frequently, and at first was careful whom she went out with, since she believed Hollywood was full of leeches, who, in her words, "sucked everybody dry." There were decent people cavorting in Hollywood, too, but Veronica really preferred the bad guys. Actually, however, she never could make up her mind. She turned down her conservative admirers and began hitting the party scene with such fervor that eventually she had to slow down. She recalled that sexual favors and drugs were plentiful at these all-night bashes, especially at the home of Errol Flynn, who had become Hollywood's most renowned playboy. Flynn's bed was his sanctuary, where he lured numerous women into one-night stands.

With Veronica as yet uncatchable, Flynn invited her to one of his film colony parties. Veronica later admitted that she was amazed by the wide assortment of gorgeous women and handsome men ready and waiting for action at Flynn's home. Of course, Errol was among that select group.

Errol tried his damnedest to win Veronica, only to strike out. Bored, Veronica left early, but gentleman that he always was, Flynn escorted her to the door, giving her one last chance. He gazed into her eyes, embraced her around the waist, and whispered, "Let's make use of my special bedroom tonight."

Veronica's reply was, "I have my own bedroom waiting, thank you."

Errol withdrew, kissed her chastely on the cheek, and bid Veronica adieu. They bumped into each other periodically at other parties, but from then on Flynn, surprisingly, kept his hands to himself. In fact, at a later party, Errol came to Veronica's rescue when an unnamed gentleman tried his own sexual persuasion on her. Flynn told the fellow, "You won't get far with her. Take it from me."

Teet Carle remembers that the rivalry between Veronica and her mother also extended to the subject of men, even though Mrs. Keane has reported to the contrary. As Carle says: "I remember one woman from the Paramount publicity department, who went on a bond-selling tour with Veronica, said that Veronica's mother said to her, 'You know, Veronica's supposed to be a very seductive person, but I've always been able to take any man from Veronica.' I'll never forget what Dale Rooks, a co-worker of mine, said: 'You know, I never thought I'd understand the meaning of how "some animals eat their own" until now.' "

Constance denies any such competition, but does say that people often drew their own conclusions without having all the facts. Instead, she claims that she always attracted more men than Veronica but it was because she was more outgoing—and that it was always on a conversational level. As she explains: "One time we were at Romanoff's and there were five millionaires at the table. One friend of mine said, 'You know, Connie, it's all your fault.' I said, 'What do you mean, it's my fault?' He said, 'Well, I've watched you. There are five millionaires at that table, she's (Veronica) twiddling her thumbs, and they're talking to you.' "

Veronica also became quite friendly with millionaire

Howard Hughes, who, though usually mysterious, sometimes surprised her by his actions. During one party, Lake recalled that for no particular reason Hughes, a very lonely man, pretended that he was deaf. Veronica was carrying on a conversation with State Supreme Court Judge Blake and Ambassador Pawley over one of Blake's recent court cases.

Moving her entourage to the kitchen, Veronica continued the discussion. Hughes amazed everyone when he suddenly spoke up from the living room with some additional facts on the case in question. Lake and the others grouped around the counter wondering how a deaf man could have such sharp hearing. Unfazed, Hughes returned to his deaf routine for the rest of the evening.

Veronica's ego had never been bigger. According to her own accounts, she was the most pursued and most "eligible actress in Hollywood." Admirers from all sectors of the world courted her. Ship merchant Aristotle Onassis used his affluence when trying to win the popular siren. Although it was wartime, he sent weekly care packages from Greece containing perfume, steak, wine, and nylons. But when Veronica reacted indifferently and failed to reciprocate, Onassis tried his luck elsewhere.

Her strangest romance came by telegram, however. It said:

> Will pay you 100-thousand dollars repeat
> 100-thousand dollars to marry me STOP
> Promise divorce within three repeat
> three days STOP Request immediate
> answer STOP Thank you.
>
> Tommy Manville

Veronica said later that she had been tempted to accept Manville's offer, for the money if nothing else. Her unemployment couldn't have been more ill-timed. Medical bills were more than she ever dreamed possible, totaling $25,000, and included an operation for her mother; and there were legal expenses incurred by her divorce. She was also sending her parents $115 a week, based on an agreement drafted between the three of them in October 1943. It promised that if Veronica ever made the grade in show business, she would repay her parents the amount of money they had invested in starting her career—the very same kind of agreement that would get her in trouble some years later.

It became obvious just how much Veronica needed money when *Life* magazine paid her two thousand dollars for a revealing cover story on her life. She showed absolutely no scruples whatsoever in talking about her parents, excoriating them for improperly raising her and for neglecting her as a child. But these derogatory remarks should not have come as any great surprise—Veronica was always mixing fact and fiction. Nevertheless, the article drew the wrath of the Keanes and also infuriated Paramount's head of production, Y. Frank Freeman. In the article, the writer had also interviewed director Preston Sturges on Veronica's many screen qualities. His response was welcomed by Lake, who took it as a big joke. But Freeman didn't.

As Teet Carle recalls: "The reporter interviewed Preston, who said at the time, 'One of the charms about Veronica is she has a pear-shaped ass, rather than apple-shaped.' The head of the studio was Y. Frank Freeman. He was so scandalized by this that he came into the commissary to Sturges' table where Veronica always ate with him. Freeman proceeded to bawl out Sturges, and expressed similar dissatisfaction with Veronica. Sturges took this all in stride; he always called Frank, 'Papa Freeman,' and it was Freeman who kept Sturges working years later when nobody in Hollywood would have him."

Given her financial plight, Veronica's house was put up for sale and she and Elaine moved in with Rita Beery. Rent was fifty dollars a month. Elaine was nearing her fourth birthday and missed her father; Veronica could never supply enough affection to satisfy her daughter's needs. Instead, she put some of the responsibility onto her mother, who cared for the child periodically.

Still strapped financially, Veronica was now seen wearing what some people called her "funny wardrobe," clothes whipped together by Veronica's dressmaker at a cost of no more than twenty dollars a frock. It was later revealed that the dressmaker was Veronica's mother, who once again had come to her daughter's aid. (Constance, however, was a better cook than a seamstress.) Veronica continued to actively support government war bond programs or other patriotic causes, including the USO. Teet Carle recounted one incident that reflected her financial situation:

> The studio was doing some charity drive for the USO. Everybody in the publicity department was given a roster of names and told to seek out donations from those people. I had on my list such stars as Joel McCrea, Ray Milland, Barbara Stanwyck, Claudette Colbert, Frederic March, and several others. The USO people wanted me to start out with Joel McCrea, Claudette Colbert, and Barbara Stanwyck first, asking each to pledge one hundred dollars. So I put their names down on the list and afterwards I told them, "Quite frankly, this is what you do. You give them one hundred dollars." They all said, "Okay." Then, finally, I called Veronica and explained how this drive was for the war effort and she came to see me. I handed her this sign-up sheet, which showed the first three names

and how they were each donating one hundred dollars. She very plainly took *one dollar* out of her purse and put down on the sheet, "Veronica Lake—one dollar." It didn't bother her one bit that the three people ahead of her were giving a hundred times as much.

Carle also recalls that even though Veronica loathed public appearances, when it came to war bond assemblies, she could be counted on for showing up. When Dorothy Lamour returned from her nationwide tour, officials of the war bond program asked Paramount to line up several stars to appear at Lamour's homecoming arrival at Los Angeles' Union Station. Veronica complied with Teet's request to appear, feeling that it was her patriotic duty, even though it meant a six A.M. wake-up call.

Surely Veronica would have traded some of these generous acts for a raise in salary. In those financially depressed months, the flow of booze never stopped, but her diet suffered considerably. She would never eat properly, skipping a meal or two in order to save money, but because of her excessive drinking, her weight climbed to one hundred and three pounds.

Jan Grippo, who still kept in touch with her periodically, blames Paramount for not helping her out financially. "Veronica was never properly remunerated for her performances and the amount of box-office income she generated for Paramount. There should have been a compromise. When you become a star, you assume tremendous obligations, both financially and socially. You have to have a good car. You just can't drive any ordinary car. You have to entertain people. You're a star—you're supposed to be glamorous. Without those things, you just peter out because you can't reciprocate since you're not making enough money."

With all that was happening both financially and socially, Veronica tried clamping down on what was being made public about her life. Her fans wanted to know the inside scoop on her life—who she was dating, where she was living, and where she was socializing—but Veronica believed that that was nobody's business but her own. Thus, she began to only patronize private parties or to prefer the seclusion of her own home. It was the only way she kept her sanity.

12

· · · ·

Life with Bandi

IT WAS JANUARY 1944 and
Veronica was celebrating the first anniversary of her divorce from John Detlie. It had not been a good year. With her stormy private life making headlines, Veronica's popularity began to sag. Paramount's executive staff wasn't sure what to do with her next. Buddy DaSylva, who was the head of production, reviewed Lake's future with the studio, but confessed that he doubted her appeal would last much longer now that the gimmick of her hair had begun to wane. The studio had other attractive and potential ingenues waiting in the wings: Joan Caulfield, Marjorie Reynolds, Diana Lynn, Gail Russell, Jean Heather, and Barbara Britton. Paramount believed it was wiser to start investing more in their future at this time than in Veronica's, who, even at the crest of her popularity, had always been difficult to handle.

While they pondered her future, the studio maintained its contractual obligation by casting Veronica in her next feature, *Bring on the Girls.* The film, which commenced production on January 10, 1944, was her first Technicolor film and first musical for the studio, even though she never could sing or dance. For these reasons, she had originally turned down the offer, but the studio persuaded her that it was the best property available. Veronica recalled: "At first, I didn't want to play in *Bring on the Girls.* It was a musical and whatever talents I had I thought were in dramatic lines. I can't sing. I don't dance superlatively, but they cast me in the film anyway."

Bring on the Girls, a low-budget musical, also starred Marjorie Reynolds, Eddie Bracken, and Sonny Tufts. It also introduced a new dancing star in Johnny Foy, a former Broadway hoofer. Music was by Spike Jones and his City Slickers burlesquing "Choloe," as well as the Golden Gate Quartet, who scored in *Star Spangled Rhythm*. Sidney Lanfield directed.

The film proved that Veronica's hairdo was still news, as well as the fact that her weight had climbed to a hundred and six pounds . Like the Paramount executives, she admitted that she, too, had grown tired of the hairdo. "I prefer my hair tied back. I can talk about that hair as though it is some other person. 'Veronica Lake' on the screen doesn't seem to me to be myself. I even sometimes want to reach up on the screen and yank that hair back from the girl's eye. It isn't going to keep a girl on the screen simply because she has hair over her eye."

Lake had to have a bottle of water constantly at her side during filming to keep her hair in place. The cameraman, while looking through the camera's lens, was unaccustomed to watching her hair flop over one eye. So, he borrowed a bottle of goo from the hairdressing department.

But Veronica revolted; she wanted her tresses to look soft, not plastered on. So the hairdresser supplied her with a bottle of water and told her to wet down her hair before every scene. It didn't help much, though, as the hot lights quickly dried out her hair. Admitting her frustration to a reporter on the set, she said, "I'm tired of reading about my hair."

As usual, Veronica also continued pulling the unexpected on the set. Teet Carle remembers on one occasion that she embarrassed a newspaper reporter over the way in which he was dressed. As Carle recalls:

> There was this one reporter named Barney Oldfield from Lincoln, Nebraska, who came out quite often to the studio to interview different celebrities. He was one of the flashiest dressers you've ever seen. I remember one time he came out on one of his trips to meet Veronica. He had been wearing the loudest sport coat money could buy. Now, here's Veronica, she knows nothing about him, and I walked in to her dressing room and said, "Veronica, I want you to meet Barney Oldfield." She looked at him, snarled, taking one glance at his wardrobe, and said, "My, God, did you lose a bet to make you wear that damn thing?" Barney just screamed with laughter—her remark was totally unexpected.

Another time, at three o'clock in the morning, she drove to the top of a Hollywood mountain, tiptoed to the bedroom window of a newspaper reporter, hammered violently on the window, and shouted, "This is the air raid warden—all your lights are on!" The reporter instantly leaped out of bed, awakened his slumbering wife, and stumbled through a completely dark house to find Veronica at his front door smiling elfishly.

Veronica was still quite upset over the studio's decision to cast her in a musical—and she let people know. She was heard saying many vitriolic things about people in the front office, calling them "lamebrains" or "asses" for frequently mishandling her affairs. Someone once asked Henry Ginsberg, who later replaced Buddy DaSylva, "How can you keep someone under contract who says such vicious things about you people?"

His reply was, "The kid's still selling tickets. When she stops selling, then we'll worry about it."

But trouble must have been in Veronica's genes, as she also experienced run-ins with the law. In February 1944 Municipal Judge Louis W. Kaufman issued a bench warrant for Veronica for apparently overlooking a traffic citation. Several weeks earlier, officer J. E. Haggerty had cited Lake for driving forty-two miles an hour in a twenty-five mile zone, having no registration in her sedan, and driving with faulty headlights. Veronica was ticketed at the corner of Wilshire and Crenshaw boulevards, and told the officer that she "didn't see the speedometer."

On February 17, 1944, Veronica appeared in court. Her attorney explained that Lake had not answered the summons on her traffic ticket because of "an apparent misunderstanding." The misunderstanding was never fully explained, although the judge understood enough to fine Veronica fourteen dollars and to warn her that additional fines would be levied if her registration wasn't updated and her front lights replaced.

Veronica put herself on good behavior, at least until after *The Hour Before the Dawn* premiered on March 24, 1944. (The film was her only contribution to the cinema world in 1944.) Critical reaction was mild compared to her previous screen blockbusters, though critics agreed that her death scene was cinematic beauty at its best. Dorothy

Masters summed it up in her two-and-a-half star New York *Daily News* review: "Veronica Lake is not at her best as an enemy agent, particularly when the role occasions only one glimpse of her in flowing locks and revealing night-dresses." Another reviewer was even more blunt: "The picture sinks . . . to the realm of painfully obvious melo-drama."

But the chief complaint was not about her talent but over her hidden hair. Fans voiced their dissatisfaction in hundreds of letters addressed to the studio. It was unanimous: the public wanted Veronica Lake with the peekaboo bang—it was like robbing Charlie Chaplin of his famous tramp costume and cane, leaving him with no personality.

Paramount informed her that there would be a long hiatus after *Bring on the Girls* because they had quite a large backlog of films ready for release. Because of the war, studios had stepped up production and overproduced, and, therefore, had to reduce their output. By 1945 production was down from 442 films to 377, the lowest number of films annually produced in Hollywood's history.

For a while, Veronica didn't seem to mind not working. It gave her more time to hit the Hollywood party circuit. She was also able to escape from the game of being a movie celebrity—Veronica loathed promotional and public appearances, unless they benefited the armed forces.

Surprisingly, even her financial picture finally brightened when Paramount offered Veronica a big, fat raise. Paramount's big three finally voted to up her salary proportionately with the revenue her films had brought in. She would now receive a whopping $5,000 a week and almost be on a level with Hope, Crosby, and Lamour.

Confrontations with the law continued, however. On April 6, 1944, the actress was flagged down for driving fifty-three miles an hour in a twenty-five mile zone. The officer quoted Lake as again saying, "I guess I wasn't watching the speedometer." The violation was her second in as many months.

Thirteen days later, Lake appeared in court to appeal the charge. This time Judge Kauffman wasn't as soft with his judgment as he had been with her first offense. Lake's attorney, Arthur W. Kennedy, tried to get the citation dropped, but Kauffman heavily reprimanded her, fining Veronica fifty dollars and suspending her driver's license for twenty days.

Paramount's executive board let this incident blow over, but threatened to take necessary disciplinary action if further serious violations ensued. It was bad publicity for the studio, but, more importantly, it was bad for the star's image. And Veronica's image needed all the facelifting that was available.

In June 1944, following her layoff, Paramount put Veronica back to work in another formula comedy, *Out of This World,* co-starring Eddie Bracken, Diana Lynn, Cass Daley, and Florence Bates. Hal Walker produced and directed. It was her second Technicolor film and her second with Eddie Bracken. In the picture, Lake portrays a secretary to a New York entertainment booking executive who helps a telegram boy (Eddie Bracken) become the latest teenage singing sensation. As in the previous Lake–Bracken vehicle, Veronica vies for the comedian's devotion, with the wide-eyed Diana Lynn, the leader of an all-girls band, as her main competition. Even though this picture received fairly good reviews, it never drummed up much business at the box office.

It was during the production of this film that reporters tried feretting out more information on Elaine. Up until then, she had been known to Lake fans as "the mystery girl." Nobody knew anything about her, or how well mother and daughter got along with each other. It was Veronica's wish that Elaine not be exhibited for public consumption. As she told one reporter, "I just don't like the idea." Even though she disliked being a mother and didn't want Elaine, she explained that she wanted her daughter to grow up normally. As she once said: "I know how important the first five years of a child's life are for her life-long character and I want to give Elaine the happiest kind of adult existence. I didn't, but that gives me all the more reason for wanting one for my baby. Learning obedience early seems to be most important." Of course, Veronica seldom practiced what she preached. She knew how to act like an authority on any subject, including motherhood, but her actions were often inconsistent with her professed beliefs.

Veronica told another member of the Los Angeles press corps that she didn't want Elaine following in her footsteps. She said:

> I hope my daughter never wants to take up acting. Acting itself I love. It's in my blood, but I hope it isn't in Elaine's, for I never want her to face situations like her privacy being intruded upon. I didn't want to have to face them either, and I honestly believe if John hadn't gone in the Army, I would have quit the screen altogether. But when he did go in, there was our baby to look after and our small investments to try to protect. I only made a small salary then, so very little went toward supporting the house and child.

With John making only two hundred dollars a week as an art director at MGM, Veronica's comment would seem to bear some truth.

When hearing her daughter's confession that she

would have retired from show business for a simpler life, Constance disagreed. "Veronica was too restless. I had trouble with her ever since she was a little girl. I don't see how she could settle down and be happy in such an environment. She was a very strange child."

When *Out of This World* concluded production in September 1944, Paramount showed that it still had Veronica's best interests at heart (at her new salary, they were also looking after their own) when they starred her in *Miss Susie Slagle's*. Set in 1910, the film was a better-than-average melodrama in which Lake starred as Nan Rogers, a young student nurse who falls in love with a medical intern (Pat Phelan). The story, based on a novel by Augusta Tucker, was shaped around the trials and tribulations of medical students.

The film co-starred Sonny Tufts, Ray Collins, and Lloyd Bridges, and introduced Joan Caulfield. It also marked Lillian Gish's return to the screen after several years absence. As his first feature under his new contract with Paramount, John Houseman produced; John Beery directed.

Houseman once commented on the screen adaptation. "Most of the book's sentimentality had been removed. It turned into a rather commonplace medical story along the lines of *Men in White* or *Young Doctor Kildaire.*"

Miss Susie Slagle's was also the first of two films to star Caulfield opposite Veronica. With another blonde on the set, there was considerable talk about Lake feeling very insecure. And according to Helene Nielsen that was true. "I think she did. I think it was a normal feeling for her. The business was very competitive, and it was natural for someone to say they had someone who they thought was better."

While Caulfield may have posed some type of threat in terms of sexuality, actress Julie Gibson believes that she was no match for Veronica as a box office draw. "I really don't think so. I don't think that the studio thought of her that way either. Joan Caulfield was nothing like Veronica. She didn't have the sexiness that Veronica had, or the mystique. Veronica had a special quality, while Joan Caulfield looked too healthy and wholesome."

A few days before production ceased, Buddy DaSylva suffered a heart attack so serious he had to step down as head of studio production. His successor was Henry Ginsberg.

While production moved along smoothly, director Hal Walker requested Veronica's services again in a cameo role for his new feature, *Duffy's Tavern,* which commenced filming two weeks after *Miss Susie Slagle's.* Based on the popular radio show of the same title, the film was another all-star vehicle that utilized almost every contract star on the lot: Barry Sullivan, Bing Crosby, Marjorie Reynolds, Dorothy Lamour, Betty Hutton, Robert Benchley, Paulette Goddard, Brian Donlevy, and others. Veronica appeared with Alan Ladd in an amusing blackout sketch that had them rehearsing a murder-mystery radio script.

The most important development during the shooting of *Miss Susie Slagle's* was that Veronica met André De Toth. (Veronica later gave him the nickname "Bandi.") De Toth had been a moderately successful film director at Columbia Pictures and was now employed at United Artists. He made his first bid for a career in show business in his native land of Hungary at the age of sixteen. His parents, Mikols and Vilma De Toth, were descendants of a long line of distinguished civil servants and public officials. After attending law college at the University of Hungary, De Toth performed as an actor in a traveling stock company, using an assumed name. His first film as a director was *Passport to Suez* (1943), followed by *None Shall Escape* (1944), both at Columbia.

At the time of their meeting, André had just wrapped

up his first film for United Artists, *Dark Waters,* and was preparing to cast his second feature, *Dishonored Lady.* Originally, De Toth wanted to meet Veronica to offer her the lead in the picture. But after he secured the introduction, he became enamored of her. Eventually he asked her out to dinner.

According to Lake, it was not love at first sight when she first met André. As she once explained:

> We dated for three whole months, after our mutual agent, Vic Orsatti, introduced us, before so much as the thought of romance ever crossed our minds. We were, in fact, opposed to romance, though for different reasons. I had been divorced and felt pretty disillusioned on the subject of marriage. Bandi had never been married and believed himself to be a confirmed bachelor. We started dating very casually, once a week or so, then twice a week, then several nights a week, than every night. The thing that kept drawing us more and more together was that we were having so much fun in one another's company.

In late November, after Veronica started her third picture, *Hold That Blonde,* De Toth asked her to marry him. She accepted, and they set their wedding date for December 13, 1944.

Known around Hollywood as "Mr. Cyclops," because of the loss of vision in one eye, De Toth was also considered to be a macho type with a temperament to match. Veronica admitted even before the wedding that whenever they argued, André would slug her in the mouth and afterward take a carving knife and tell her to cut out his tongue in revenge. But she was obviously deeply in love, and too afraid to challenge him.

Life magazine was ready to cover the De Toth–Lake wedding—Veronica's picture on the cover sold millions of copies every time. A reporter and photographer were both assigned to the story, but cancelled out on orders from above at the last minute. As Constance recalls: "*Life* magazine was going to cover the wedding when she was marrying De Toth, but when they heard that I wasn't invited, nobody showed up. There was a time when *Life* didn't go to bed without a picture of Veronica on the cover, because she was hot stuff."

It's not known who called *Life* to inform them that the Keanes had not been invited, but it was no secret that Veronica's mother was furious over the wedding. Constance had very few kinds words to say about De Toth. For one thing, he never had the courtesy to ask for her daughter's hand in marriage or to meet her family. Instead, he proposed to Veronica as if the Keanes didn't even exist.

Mrs. Keane was also concerned over De Toth's background. She had discovered some years earlier that he had been a member of the pro-Nazi movement in America. At the time, he lived on the same block as the Keanes on Doheny Boulevard. His activities in support of the German Reich often took place in his backyard, and Mrs. Keane had witnessed these demonstrations when she visited a neighbor who lived in the same apartment building as De Toth. As Constance once recounted: "Some people told me he was a Nazi. He and four other boys used to live in an apartment and worked on the docks of Los Angeles. He was very pro-Hitler at the time and he would go through all these gymnastics in his backyard, the goosestepping and all of that. There were some pro-Nazi people in the film industry, too, but many of them ended up leaving the country."

Despite her objection, the wedding went on as planned. Even Hedda Hopper stuck her nose into this major event to find out exactly when Veronica was tying the knot for the second time. Hopper reported: "I just learned the exact time of Veronica Lake's marriage to André De Toth will be 7:30 tomorrow at the home of Mr. and Mrs. Ed Gardner of Bel Air."

Her article was dated December 13, 1944, and reported that the wedding was to take place the next day when, actually, it happened that evening. It's believed that Veronica's mother received one call from Hopper, but because of her dislike for the columnist, told her the wrong date.

Both André and Veronica were working practically right up till the moment they said "I do." In fact, she had only one hour off all day, an hour in which to get her hair done. But from the day they announced their engagement, André and Veronica snatched what few free moments they could find to shop for a house and furniture. Only on the afternoon of their wedding did they finally buy a house in the Hollywood Hills area.

Thirty-five friends were present when a Beverly Hills judge performed the ceremony. Veronica, who was now twenty-two, wore a long, ice-blue crepe dress designed by one of her closest friends, Edith Head. She carried a bouquet of tiny butterfly orchids, specially ordered by André from New York.

Behind Veronica, as matron of honor, was her dearest friend, Rita Beery, her good looks augmented by an exquisite gray outfit, also designed by Head. Beery obviously had mixed emotions about the ceremony, as she was losing a friend, and more importantly, a close companion. Losing Veronica was like losing part of her life.

The moment Veronica's eyes fastened on her betrothed, she grinned broadly. It was the moment they had both been waiting for. André was tall, handsome, muscular, and splendid in his black tuxedo.

Teet Carle, who also attended, described the wedding. "I remember the staircase Veronica came down to meet André at the bottom. But when they were ready to start, she was in position but nobody could find De Toth. They found out that at the last minute, he'd decided to go to the bathroom. People kidded, 'Gee, there's one bridegroom who isn't nervous.'"

According to Carle, De Toth kept denying any wedding plans to members of the news media right up to the minute of the ceremonies. "I can remember Veronica telling newspaper people beforehand how they were going to be married, but he would stand in the back, waving his hands and whispering loud enough for everyone to hear, 'No, no, no!'"

Veronica was hopeful that she had finally found the right man. She believed he would meet her needs as a husband, and, at the same time, look after her future. Some pessimists believed André wasn't that man.

13

· · · ·

Starting Over

*N*ow that she was married, Veronica no longer had to live life in the fast lane and could focus her attention on where her life and career were heading. De Toth promised to be her guardian angel. He vowed that he would shop around for good, solid properties in which she could star, as Paramount was steadily losing interest in offering her top-of-the-line stories.

As in many career marriages, André and Veronica found little time to be alone with each other during the first few months. In fact, one month after their wedding, in January 1945, Veronica was invited to the White House for President Roosevelt's birthday party. Festivities would include a lavish Birthday Ball with a special stage production entitled *Dear Ruth,* featuring many Hollywood personalities, to precede the ball.

Bad weather forced Veronica's flight to land prematurely in Kansas City, however, and she missed the play, arriving in Washington at 2 A.M. By then, the celebration was over. And President Roosevelt left the next morning to attend a conference in Yalta. Although she never met FDR, Veronica was introduced that afternoon to Eleanor Roosevelt at an informal luncheon in the west wing of the White House. She sat next to Harry Truman's daughter, Margaret, for most of the time and later chatted with Mrs. Roosevelt about her career and new marriage.

The White House photographer organized several group shots of Mrs. Roosevelt with Myrna Loy, Gale Storm, and Margaret O'Brien, who had also made the trip. After lunch Veronica was left alone with the First Lady in another room of the White House. Eleanor appeared distraught when Veronica walked in. Veronica sensed that something was wrong, but felt it wasn't her place to pry. She didn't have to. Mrs. Roosevelt quietly announced, "The President is ill, Veronica. He has cancer of the prostate gland." Eleanor kept her back to Veronica as she spoke, staring vacantly through the Victorian-style window.

Choosing her words carefully, Veronica said, "I'm sorry, Mrs. Roosevelt, I'm sorry."

In her usual stoic manner, Eleanor replied, "Thank you, Veronica, for being so understanding. I had to tell someone. I'm sorry it was you. But you have to promise me that you won't tell anyone. It isn't in the best security interests of our country."

Wondering why Mrs. Roosevelt had selected her as her confidante, Veronica promised that she would not say a thing to anyone. Relieved, Eleanor smiled and walked Veronica out to the Rose Garden, continuing to chat about less weighty subjects until Veronica departed for the hotel.

Three months later, on April 12, 1945, Americans received news that Franklin Delano Roosevelt had died.

When she heard the grim news, Veronica's heart went out to Mrs. Roosevelt; FDR's death would put a burden on the nation, but her thoughts were with the proud woman who had been his wife.

Veronica returned to Hollywood just in time to receive the bad news about her latest box office release. *Bring on the Girls* opened on February 17, 1945. For the first time, filmgoers would have a taste of "the peekaboo girl" in Technicolor. But the film received such bad reviews that it was quickly condemned as Veronica's worst film.

In the film, she plays Teddy Collins, a cigarette girl, who works in a fashionable nightclub. Her hair is down to her shoulders and over one eye, which undoubtedly pleased her fans. Her love interest in the film is Eddie Bracken, who joins the navy; Sonny Tufts is the tough sailor in charge. However, Veronica's lines were as insipid as the film's storyline and provided her with little to do.

Despite this temporary career setback, Veronica remained undaunted. She had anticipated that *Bring on the Girls* was not her kind of vehicle, but had taken the part to appease her Paramount mentors. Paramount also realized that it was a waste of her talents when it was too late— box-office figures were the lowest of any film she had done thus far.

Hoping to set her career back on track, Paramount decided to fall back on the successful formula that had catapulted Veronica to fame. She was teamed with Alan Ladd for the third time in *The Blue Dahlia*, based on the popular novel by Raymond Chandler. The management of Paramount had also come to the horrifying realization that Ladd would be entering the army in the next three months, leaving them without a picture of Ladd in reserve, thus prompting the move.

Veronica played the character of Joyce Harwood; her

co-stars included William Bendix, Tom Powers, William Wright, Howard DaSilva, Doris Dowling, and Frank Faylen. It was the second and last picture John Houseman produced, and the second time George Marshall directed Veronica. Shooting started on March 26, 1945.

John Houseman remembers that Ladd had suggested Lake for the female lead. "Ladd now had some say in the choice of the persons with whom he worked. Since he himself was extremely short, he had only one standard by which he judged his fellow players. During casting, if another actor or actress rose above his collarbone, he was sure to explain that he didn't think he or she was right. Veronica was the perfect size for him."

Houseman also said that even though Doris Dowling was a full six inches taller than Ladd, he placated the actor in their scenes together by keeping her sitting or lying down.

Veronica continued her "aloof but friendly rapport" with Ladd, keeping her social activities with Alan and Sue to a minimum. She also continued to talk on subjects she knew little about, convincing even the authorities that she had studied her subject well. Teet Carle remembers that this included background on Raymond Chandler mystery novels, even though she had never read one in her life:

Raymond Chandler was sort of a tin god to everybody. He had written *The Blue Dahlia*, and I remember Veronica saying to me, "Who's this guy, Chandler?" I said, "Why, Veronica, he's the greatest mystery writer around." I told her all about him, and she listened and listened and listened. A couple of days later, I heard some newspaper reporter interviewing her, and she began telling him all about Raymond Chandler. She hadn't read any of his books, but remembered everything I told her. She must have had a good memory, because afterwards the reporter was convinced that she knew plenty about writers like Chandler.

Veronica preferred her role in *The Blue Dahlia* to her indifferent part in the flop *Bring on the Girls,* but although she liked Ladd, she had reservations about being linked professionally with him. She believed the frequency of their film appearances together weakened her solo film performances. As she remarked: "I didn't like becoming a team. Ladd and Lake, like MacDonald and Eddy, or Powell and Loy. I believe if once you get established that way, it seems to work out that the members of the team, broken up, are never as successful as individuals. So after I made two pictures in succession with Alan, and they suggested casting me in a third, I objected. It was nothing against Alan, whom I'm very fond of as a person."

But she really had no choice in the matter. The Ladd–Lake combo spelled big box office and the studio reminded its glamourous star that they were in the business for only one reason: to make money. Veronica was also in the business for the same reason. Her new salary enabled her to live as extravagantly as she liked, and there was security down the road because of her iron-clad contract.

Then in March 1945, Veronica learned that she was pregnant with her first child by André. The news made André extremely happy. He very much wanted a son, so much so, in fact, that he became obsessed with the idea. He would talk about having a son for hours on end, telling his wife, "I want a boy, Ronni. I really want a boy. I have to have one." André's unrealistic expectations caused Veronica to wonder if she was going to have to pack her bags if she failed to deliver him a son. Thus, when the pressure of his mandate became too intense, her family physician told De Toth to back off. Dr. McBurney advised the Hungarian director that even he would have no control over genetic destiny. As he explained, "You'll get what you get."

For a while, André tried to accept the doctor's advice, but then he grew restless and took up his demands again. "You have Elaine," he would tell Lake. "She's a very beautiful girl. Well, I'm getting my beautiful boy—and you will deliver him to me." Veronica didn't know how to cope. Withdrawing, she turned back to the bottle to soothe her anxieties and blot André's talk about having a son out of her mind.

André was equally obstinate over what to name him. He wanted André Anthony Michael De Toth III, quite a mouthful for any child. Veronica thought it was unfair to name the baby after his father because it would only add unwanted pressure to the child later in his life. They finally settled on one name: Michael.

Despite her pregnancy, Veronica managed to successfully complete filming *The Blue Dahlia* on time. Because the studio still had an enormous backlog of films ready for distribution, Paramount placed her on an extended leave of absence with pay for the rest of her pregnancy.

Lake grew restless around the house; she wasn't comfortable with the inactivity—she really needed work to structure her life. And, now in her third pregnancy, she was still distraught over the prospects of mothering another child. This time she didn't make any rash attempts to abort the baby's life; instead, she fought off her anxieties and morning sickness by drinking several shots of vodka daily. André didn't oppose her drinking at first. A heavy drinker himself, he thought it would help make the baby become big and strong.

Veronica remained secluded from the public until news of her son's birth rocketed across the nation. Louella Parsons broke the news in her column, dated October 26, 1945:

> Last evening, the peekaboo girl, Veronica Lake, presented her husband, director André De Toth, with a son. The baby was born at Good Samaritan Hospital. Veronica and her husband had both hoped earnestly for a boy. And I'm happy to report that both father and child are doing nicely. The baby, named Michael, weighed 5 pounds, 6 ounces at birth.

De Toth, in getting Veronica to the hospital, had all the makings of Hollywood's version of a hysterical father. On the evening of October 24th, André asked Veronica how she was feeling. She supposedly replied, "I want to get a lot of sleep tonight, because tomorrow is your son's birthday." At noon the following day, André drove Veronica to the hospital where Dr. McBurney was waiting. De Toth remarked, "We've come for the birth of my son."

In a slow-burn reminiscent of Edgar Kennedy, McBurney glared at André, saying, "Veronica, I think you should take this madman to lunch. Come back this afternoon."

It was André who was going through the labor pains. He had rushed his wife to the hospital early in anticipation of the big moment, only to find out it was a false alarm. The De Toths lunched at the Restaurant LaRue and, then, at approximately 3:30, Veronica began having her first labor pains and mustered up a plea: "We'd better go."

About an hour and a half hour later, Dr. McBurney emerged smiling from the operating room. André enthused, "Don't tell me, it's a son."

"All right," McBurney retorted, "have it your way."

Veronica wasn't as elated. She recalled that the first day she peered into young Michael's eyes, she knew he would become a problem child. They showed the same fiery redness she saw in André's eyes whenever he got mad. Later, she expressed her feelings to André, but he dismissed it as merely female foolishness.

14

· · · ·

A Step Backward

*T*HE YEARS 1946–1947 brought
the slow decline of Veronica's worldwide popularity. With
the increasing abandonment of her peekaboo bang, and no
new smashing assignments, filmgoers began losing interest
and shifting their attention to other up-and-coming glamour queens, including Joan Caulfield, Diana Lynn, and
Mary Hatcher, all of whom were also under contract at
Paramount and posed equal threats to Lake's popularity.

Veronica's devil-may-care attitude was partly responsible. In her current crop of films, she seemed to be going
through the motions without taking them seriously. She
continued coming to work drunk and was constantly being
sent home to sober up. Money worries were the main cause
of her reliance on the bottle, although she may have
crossed over from being a heavy drinker to becoming an
alcoholic. André put no limit on his spending. As in his

bachelor days, he enjoyed spending money, in this case Veronica's money, to buy himself frivolous things for his own enjoyment. And Veronica never had been a good money manager.

As Veronica's drinking picked up, her mother finally intervened. She enlisted the services of Father McGovern from the Good Sheperd Catholic Church in Beverly Hills and she and McGovern convinced Veronica to swear off drinking. The studio was coming down on her increasingly bizarre behavior and was itself planning to investigate. Veronica saw reason, and didn't touch a drop of alcohol for six months. During that time, her mother remembers, "For the first time, she acted like a human being." Even George Brown, head of Paramount's publicity department, credited Mrs. Keane for the turnaround. Phoning Constance, he said, "Whatever you've done with her, we're very thankful." Brown reported that Veronica was finally behaving herself and seemed happier with her work.

It is believed that Veronica's drinking resumed when her career began taking a nose dive. Certainly the release of her third and final film with Eddie Bracken, *Hold That Blonde,* didn't help. Released on November 23, 1945, two days before Thanksgiving, this lightweight comedy couldn't have been issued at a more appropriate time—it was definitely "a turkey." Formerly titled *Good Intentions,* this film was flatter and duller than the two previous Lake–Bracken features, with Bracken playing a timid but well-to-do man afflicted with kleptomania. His psychiatrist prescribes only one remedy: having romance with another woman. Bracken falls in love all right, but with an innocent member (Veronica Lake) of a jewel-robbery gang out to swipe the Romanoff necklace. Only one ingredient was missing: the comedy. Howard Barnes of the *New York Her-*

ald-Tribune wrote: "Veronica Lake postures as the walking cure for the unwilting and unwilling pickpocket (Eddie Bracken). . . . Her performance is unstable for its lack of conviction or variety of make-believe."

Veronica found some solace in her first Christmas at home with André, Elaine, and young Michael. The living room was festive with the usual yuletide trimmings, including a big Christmas tree heavily decorated with a rainbow of bulbs and lights. André and Veronica stayed up late the night before, playing Santa's role. Even though Michael was too young to understand, Veronica wanted to introduce him royally to this grand old tradition.

Two weeks before, André had received news that he was becoming an official citizen of the United States. Since his marriage to Veronica meant he would be making his home in America permanently, he had filed for citizenship earlier in the year. De Toth posed with his wife for newspaper photographers outside the Los Angeles County Records Office, proudly waving a copy of his citizenship papers. Lake wore her hair underneath a crushed velvet hat and was dressed for the occasion in a leopard coat and black satin dress. André was equally dapper in a blue suede sports jacket and tie. They looked like a loving and happy couple.

With the arrival of 1946, Paramount was still unsure over Veronica's future. Two of her films were scheduled for release that year, *Miss Susie Slagle's* and *The Blue Dahlia*, which was her lowest output ever. Prior to this, she had been averaging about four films per season. The writing was all too clearly on the wall: Veronica was being eased out.

It became even more obvious when Veronica discovered that her dressing room had been taken over by another actress. During her reign as one of Paramount's top stars, she had always maintained her own private dressing room, one of about ten or so apartment-sized rooms strung together on the bottom floor of a three-story building. Each additional story housed locker-style dressing rooms for the contract players and the studio technicians. The first deck of rooms belonged to the studio's top stars: Betty Hutton, Bing Crosby, Ray Milland, Bob Hope, Dorothy Lamour, Fred MacMurray, Frederic March, among others.

These dressing rooms featured spacious bathrooms, living rooms, sitting quarters, a bar, a kitchen, and other comforts. In addition, stars belonging to this top bracket were also able to drive and park their flashy automobiles on the backlot, whereas the contract stars had to find parking spaces outside the grounds and walk in to work.

Well, as the scuttlebutt went, Joan Caulfield was exactly the type of actress to do anything to get ahead. Her personal link to the studio's power structure was Bing Crosby, who was a major stockholder in the company. Gossip has it that Caulfield became very cozy with Crosby at the time his wife Dixie was dying of cancer.

Julie Gibson remembers that Caulfield's struggle for power ended with Veronica's dressing room. "Joan Caulfield was a pushy person and she got what she wanted. Very soon after this, I saw that Veronica's name had been mysteriously removed from her dressing room. The name that went up in its place was Joan Caulfield's, which made me very sad since I didn't like what Caulfield had done. Veronica hadn't done anything to hurt anyone."

Richard Webb, who worked with Veronica and was also under contract at Paramount, also remembers hearing about the Caulfield incident: "Joan Caulfield was a very, very, very close friend and confidante of Bing Crosby's. She was an endlessly striking girl, but she couldn't act. She did what she had to do if she wanted something badly enough."

Several attempts were made to contact Miss Caulfield on the accuracy of these stories, but she has refused to comment. It should be postscripted, however, that Veronica fought tooth-and-nail with the studio brass and acquired another first-class dressing room shortly thereafter. Otherwise, she didn't comment on the situation to the press or even to Caulfield. Instead, she showed her resentment toward Caulfield during their first meeting while filming *Miss Susie Slagle's*. Paramount had been hyping Caulfield as the studio's "sensational new discovery," but Veronica acted indifferently during filming of the scenes between them, walking through her performance "as though she were in a trance."

Julie Gibson recalls that Veronica knew that some of the people at the studio cared about her and about her well-being, such as Edith Head and Bill Miekeljohn, Paramount's talent department head, but that that didn't include the studio hierarchy. With dollars at stake, Paramount seemed to prefer promoting its attractive young actresses with as much spunk but fewer personal problems than Lake. Besides, Veronica's popularity with the public was fading. As Julie Gibson relates:

> There's a lot of studio protocol that goes on. You have to be ready when they want you and jump when they want you. They might want you to go out with a young contract player and act as his escort for the evening, either to a preview or special screening of a new movie. At first, these social events were fun, until they become deadly dull and boring to do. After a while, it was very easy to say, "No," that you had something else to do, that you had a toothache, things like that. Veronica didn't want these things anymore, since she had done her full share.

Ironically, on the heels of the Lake–Caulfield controversy, their film together, *Miss Susie Slagle's,* was issued to theaters from Cucamonga to Key Largo on March 8, 1946. The film received modest reviews, with some critics citing Lake's performance as listless. Lee Mortimer of the *Daily Mirror* complained that "in the action department the film falls down. There's no more of that commodity than is naturally found in a dissecting room. In other words, it's stiff." Howard Barnes of the *New York Herald-Tribune* had this to say: "*Miss Susie Slagle's* is leisurely entertainment, but it has a great deal of authenticity, considerable feeling and not a little engaging comedy." Despite these mixed reviews, *Miss Susie Slagle's* was named "Box Office Champion of the Month" by Quigley Publications, which published several fan magazines at the time.

At least one film series was Veronica's saving grace in Hollywood—her films with Alan Ladd. *The Blue Dahlia* proved why when it opened on April 19, 1947. The film was "a taut and exciting" thriller about a discharged navy flier (Alan Ladd) who discovers his wife (Doris Dowling) has been unfaithful. When she is murdered, he is implicated and must find the culprit. In his search for evidence, he meets up with Joyce Harwood (Veronica Lake), the separated wife of club owner Howard Da Silva.

The Blue Dahlia made not only "a heap of money" for Paramount, but attracted critical kudos from every coast, such as the following from Bosley Crowther of *The New York Times:* "Paramount has contributed a honey of a rough 'em up romance that goes by the name of *The Blue Dahlia* . . . it makes for a brisk and exciting show." *The Blue Dahlia* equaled the success of *This Gun for Hire,* the first Ladd–Lake feature, posting over $10 million in revenue. Veronica and Alan could still draw crowds as one of the screen's greatest romantic teams.

Following this screen triumph, Veronica and André decided to put their Hollywood Hills home up for sale and buy a twenty-three acre ranch in Chatsworth, which was thirty-five miles east of the San Fernando Valley area. In May 1946 the De Toths plunked down three hundred thousand dollars for the property. It featured rolling hills, stables for horses, and plenty of acreage for growing crops. André also bought a vacation house in the mountain resort area of Bishop, California.

Helene Nielsen, who moved in with the De Toths when they relocated to the Chatsworth ranch, recalls that it was a beautiful piece of property, but costly to maintain. "It took a lot of money for the upkeep. I think that's why they were both working to pay off the debt they had gotten into. Veronica liked the outdoors and wasn't the type who wanted a big house, the big parties, and didn't want to appear like a big show-off."

Nielsen remembers that the Chatsworth ranch was "a rambling sort of house" with three bedrooms, a large living room, a modern kitchen, and three bathrooms. The dining room was separate from the kitchen, and Veronica hired a maid and one servant to help maintain the household.

According to Nielsen, Veronica and André once tried raising wheat to make money, but they were never home to properly supervise harvesting the crop. "They kept working so much that they were hardly home. When they did come home, they were tired and went to bed. I was usually with the nurse and Elaine when they weren't home, doing errands."

The Chatsworth ranch was everything Veronica had hoped for. As she once said: "We want a place with a pool and room for a couple of horses and lots of dogs. But what we won't have is an 'estate.' The place will be no bigger than what one good cook-maid, a nurse, and I can keep up."

When André and Veronica purchased the property, there weren't any floors in the place, or trees on the premises. The rest of the landscape was underdeveloped with the exception of the foundation for the stables. But Veronica kept her promise to fill the ranch to capacity with livestock. She owned four Doberman pinschers, chickens, rabbits, ducks, and two horses. The Chatsworth ranch became her peaceful hideaway from the daily anxieties of Hollywood.

Veronica had very little time to devote to fixing up the ranch as André was arranging last-minute preparations for *Ramrod,* his first film with his wife. The film was being produced through an independent company, Enterprise Productions. André was to direct Veronica for the first time as well. In June 1946 *Ramrod* began location filming near Zion National Park in Utah. Cast to star opposite Lake were Joel McCrea, Donald Crisp, Charlie Ruggles, Don DeFore, and Preston Foster. It was the first time McCrea had worked with Veronica since *Sullivan's Travels.*

But, according to Veronica, the production was marred by setbacks from the very beginning. On the tenth day of shooting, she injured herself slightly when a horse shied away and stepped on her ankle. Veronica was out for about a week. Then, thirteen days later, the Associated Press wire service reported that a fire had swept through the set of *Ramrod:*

A fire scene in the motion picture *Ramrod* became the real thing today as a swift wind whipped the flames, endangering Joel McCrea, Veronica Lake, and others on location here. . . . McCrea, who co-stars with Miss Lake, singed his hands helping battle the flames, which swept from a purposely ignited barn across the set to a ranch-house. Miss Lake was to have been in the house but ran to safety when McCrea and others rid-

ing on horseback toward the building were stopped by
the heat.

Misfortune struck again on July 25, 1946. Veronica was
flown home when she came down with pneumonia and a
hundred-and-four degree temperature. Her doctor admin-
istered pencillin and she was back on location a week later,
glad to finish up filming.

André's temperamental behavior was also at issue on
the set. De Toth was in the throes of a mutiny with his cast
and crew over "technical differences." André was a very
physical director and sometimes used shock tactics to make
his actors follow his commands. This included telling an
actor if he didn't do a scene right, he would never work in
Hollywood again. And Veronica would side with her husband one moment, then shift to the side of the actors.
Veronica admitted several years later that De Toth's occasional temper tantrums had resulted in his losing several
jobs with his former employers, including Enterprise Productions.

When *Ramrod* completed production in mid-Septem-
ber, Paramount reached back into its script department and
pulled out *Saigon.* The film would become the weakest of
the Ladd–Lake series. Veronica later recalled: "By this
time, working with Alan was like carrying on a conversation
with an old friend. There was no surprises between us and
no friction. We continued our aloof but friendly relationship and it was smooth sailing all the way."

Saigon was the first directorial assignment at Paramount for newcomer Leslie Fenton. Fenton, a former
actor, had made his impact in the same kind of tough-guy
characterizations for which Ladd was noted. The film also
brought about an acting reunion for Luther Adler and Morris Carnovsky, both of whom were prominently associated

with the Group Theatre during its years on Broadway. *Saigon* also featured a young actor named Douglas Dick.

Dick recalls that Veronica "was pretty remote. I never got to know her, personally. We never became friends, never had lunch together, or anything. I'd have to admit that I didn't find her that interesting. She didn't seem terribly gifted in the head. But she was cooperative and cool. She was never mean to me, or anyone, nor was she helpful from what I could see." Dick added that there was never any closeness on the set between members of the cast like there was with other acting teams. "Even between Alan and her, there wasn't that usual professional camaraderie that you've seen between people who've worked together a lot. There wasn't a kind of playfulness. Everybody worked and that was it."

It was also apparent that Lake's peekaboo hairstyle had lost some of its appeal with the public. Douglas Dick agrees: "I think her hairdo was important to her career, until it just got to be an old gimmick. But what really furthered her career was the fact that she worked so well with Alan Ladd. I think the two things together helped her. She was small, Alan was small, and Paramount needed someone to work in that way. And she did the trick."

It has also been learned that co-star Luther Alder was infatuated with Veronica, and was hoping to spark a romance between them. But Veronica now feared the consequences of having an affair—especially if André ever found out, as he was much stronger both emotionally and physically than she was. Where John Detlie failed, André succeeded. He was firmer with Veronica and often gave her a swift kick in the pants when she needed it. He could be compassionate at times, but he knew how to manipulate his wife.

Filming of *Saigon* came to a close on January 25, 1947.

About a month before, however, Veronica's up and down relationship with Anthony Keane had come to an abrupt end. On December 10, 1946, she received word that her stepfather had died of a heart attack. Keane succumbed while attending a musicale in the home of composer Sidon Lane. Rosary services were held the following day at 8 P.M. and Keane's body was later flown to Brooklyn, New York, where he was interred.

Veronica attended neither the flower or rosary service, and never sent even a single bouquet of flowers in sympathy. Although her feelings about Anthony had been ambivalent, especially when she was growing up, the general feeling was that she had been fond of him. She was again not communicating with her mother and perhaps just didn't want to be bothered with Constance's problems in addition to her own. Constance has expressed bitterness over her daughter's actions, saying that it was "totally irresponsible of her." It would have been the least she could have done, according to Mrs. Keane.

Evidently, Veronica thought otherwise.

Paramount glamour shot used to publicize Lake's peekaboo
image.

Right: With Joel McCrea from *Sullivan's Travels.* Veronica was dressed in baggy clothes to hide the fact she was pregnant.

Below: Having fun in the snow with William ("Hopalong Cassidy") Boyd in upstate New York.

Above: This mid-forties portrait best illustrates the Veronica Lake mystique.

Right: With Alan Ladd from *The Blue Dahlia.*

Above: Lake and Joan Caulfield were usually at opposite ends, including still sessions for *The Sainted Sisters*.

Above left: Veronica with her second husband, André De Toth. *(credit: Jeff Lenburg Collection)*

Left: Veronica's three children, Michael, Diane, and Elaine on the Chattsworth ranch. *(credit: Constance Keane)*

Veronica with Alan Ladd and Douglas Dick from the last
Ladd–Lake feature, *Saigon*.

Below: With Nat Perlow, who
supported Veronica after her split
from her third husband, Joe McCarthy.
(credit: Constance Keane)

Lake backstage from *Best Foot Forward* at Stage 73 in New York in 1963.

Revisiting her star on the Hollywood Walk of Fame in 1971, with *Hollywood Reporter* columnist, Sue Cameron, and entertainer, Gary Owens. *(credit: Gary Owens)*

15

····

Trouble in Paradise

BY 1947, LIFE at the Chatsworth ranch was no longer Shangri-la. Serious financial problems began to surface with increasing frequency and André's free-spending ways cut off any chances of saving. Despite their rather substantial combined incomes, André was financially irresponsible, spending their money freely and consistently.

Sometimes, after he had accepted a new film project, André would become livid over something trivial and would storm off the set, never to return. The studio in question usually ordered him off the lot and and gave him his walking papers. It was less hazardous for everyone involved to hire a new director than to have De Toth continue to behave badly. This started happening more often than not and finally, Veronica's Paramount salary became their only source of income. When he chose to, André really knew how to manipulate people; some believe he would have made a better used-car salesman than a director.

But it was how André spent their money that annoyed Veronica. After they moved into the ranch, De Toth complained one afternoon about the dimensions of the living room, flatly stating that it was two feet too small. He also disliked the room's color scheme: Chinese red and white, Veronica's favorite colors. He told his wife that it looked more like a barn than a room in which to entertain family and guests. So André hired a team of building contractors to come in and knock out the wall, adding two feet of new construction. It cost over three thousand dollars for that additional space, and although afterward he was convinced that the room looked bigger, Veronica wasn't. She vented her anger over Andre's foolishness by resorting to the bottle.

On Valentine's Day, Veronica was considering buying him a new shirt or new wallet, which was about all their budget would allow. André informed her that he was going to buy a small commercial airplane, which would be *her* gift to *him.* This two-seater craft was loaded with extras, and the price tag was a whopping ten thousand dollars. Veronica tried putting up a fight but, as usual, André won out, convincing her that they would share the plane (both of them would have to take flying lessons, an additional expense).

A week after André learned how to pilot the plane, it caught fire during a flight over Salt Lake City. The fire started in the cabin twenty-five miles east of the city when the De Toths were en route to Denver, Colorado. Grabbing her fur coat, Veronica doused the blaze while her husband swung the plane around for a safe landing at the Salt Lake City Airport. Slightly nauseated by the pungent odor of the burning fur, Lake and her husband left the plane at the airport for repairs to the burned-out radio and caught the next train to Denver. The damage totaled around five hundred dollars.

André and Veronica had been heading for Denver to attend the premiere of *Ramrod.* The film opened on February 25, 1947, in forty-one theaters in Utah as well as in an equal number in Colorado. It was announced that *Ramrod* was being tabbed the official film of Utah's Centennial celebration. The train that carried the De Toths to Denver was nicknamed the "Ramrod Special." Greeting them with a fast round of sightseeing were Utah's Governor Herbert B. Maw and Salt Lake's Mayor Earl J. Glade, who were the official hosts. Preceding the film's premiere Friday night, the Hollywood personalities participated in a mammoth parade that attracted about seventy-five thousand spectators.

Ramrod broke all house records in Utah. According to an Enterprise Productions report, thirty-two out of forty-one theaters set new one-day box office records. Most of this was the result of the state-wide promotional campaign preceding the opening of the production.

Back home, André continued to buy new goods for his own enjoyment, from Palomino horses to yachts to new automobiles. And Veronica always capitulated. He also started taking long and frequent trips to Europe and Mexico, supposedly in search of new film properties for his wife. He gained few friends when the means in which he won Veronica's financial support became known to her family and friends. As Constance remembers: "He would get her drunk so that he would get the things he wanted, Palomino horses, yachts, and his Navion airplane."

Helene Nielsen has said that her cousin was like "a rag doll" under his power. "She was like a puppet on a string. She should have met with an attorney and said, 'Look, this is my money and I want it protected for my future.' But she didn't. She listened to him. He knew how to feed her, and knew how to make promises he'd never keep. One day, he'd say, 'You're wonderful,' building her up and making her feel good before downing her. She just never fought back. Fear had a lot to do with that. She was afraid of him. He just overwhelmed her.''

Richard Webb remembers the perils of challenging the fiery Hungarian:

> I was of a stature to be included in his coterie. He was a gung-ho, macho type, and he was a pilot. When I learned to fly, he asked me if I wanted to join the Q-Bs [Quiet Birdmen]. That sounded like fun, at first. André was acting as bartender and everybody drank as much as they could possibly put away, I guess to prove that they were macho. If they had a new person, they tried to get him as drunk as possible as fast as possible. André tried buying me with some line on, "If you're a real Q-B, you'll drink with us." I told him what he could do with his Q-Bs, because I remember he had this wild, crazed look in his eyes. He was ready to kill me, but I thought twice about it. As it turned out, I didn't qualify for the Q-Bs because I just couldn't put up with his macho stuff.

Veronica began to feel trapped. She was more like a prisoner than an occupant. Her schizophrenic condition had progressed to the point that she started feeling persecuted because André wouldn't let her friends come over to visit. He still acted as if he were a confirmed bachelor, with Veronica on hand to serve as his banker. He invited his own friends over regularly for drinks, including producer Ivan Tors, Sabu, and Charles Wittinger. Veronica never really socialized with them, but, like an automaton, she obeyed André's command to join them temporarily.

She would stare vacantly at the surroundings, then, obviously feeling unaccepted, she would excuse herself and go to her room.

The severity of her schizophrenic illness really became noticeable at this point in her life. She was so withdrawn that her only escape was to sit in her room and listen daily to Miklos Rozsa's soundtrack of *Spellbound.* She preferred this bizarre but faithful recording to watching television, according to Helene Nielsen, replaying it as her only means of entertainment. There was a good reason, however, as this recording was just another link to her schizophrenia. She related to the story that dealt with powerful human emotions—the struggle of a great love against the disrupting pressure of a man's paranoiac fantasies. That love, between a woman doctor and her patient, is clearly expressed in the stirring theme of the concerto's opening moments, building to the hero's paranoiac attack on the doctor. It is believed that Veronica related to the intensity of this story, finding some solace in the chaotic twists this recording takes and realizing that others suffered similarly.

Veronica also drank heavily during this period, but consumption of alcohol made her feel only more insecure, more paranoid about André and his schemes, and more afraid that the world was crushing her.

Her deep-seated agitation continued through the spring of 1947, when she began filming her second and last film with Joan Caulfield, *The Sainted Sisters.* Veronica has said that she heard through various sources that one Paramount executive supposedly wagered, "Let's put Lake in with Caulfield. Caulfield will fix her ass all right."

Veronica wisely kept a low profile on the set. Nevertheless, she got even during her performance. Executives walked out on screenings of daily rushes, shaking their heads. It was reported that every time Joan Caulfield fed

Veronica her lines, Lake would just stand there and, in the game tradition of Oliver Hardy, stare blankly at her. Some hailed Lake for her ability to steal scenes without batting an eyelash. It wasn't that at all; she simply despised Caulfield.

Caulfield wasn't amused. She reportedly left several screenings screaming a melange of obscenities about her co-star. In an interview, Joan Caulfield sugarcoated these reports, saying, "I had a very rewarding relationship with Barry Fitzgerald [another co-star] and spent my time on the set with him, and had no personal contact with Veronica, other than work-related."

The closest Caulfield came to admitting there were personality clashes between them was when she wrote the following in a letter to the author: "I do feel her [Lake's] sudden stardom, the peekaboo hairdo and her sultry sex image found her totally unprepared to cope with the reality of life and its serious responsibilities."

In the fall of 1947 Veronica and André became embroiled in all sorts of legal action. They initiated the action on October 8, 1947, when they filed two suits for a total of three thousand dollars damages in Superior Court against James Cassidy and Polan Banks who, according to the De Toths, were to have produced a film entitled, *There Goes Lona Henry*. Based on a novel written by Banks, the suit alleged that DeToth was to be paid fifty thousand dollars for directing and that Miss Lake was to receive two hundred fifty thousand dollars and twenty percent of the film's net profits for her performance, totaling half a million dollars in salaries.

But De Toth dropped the suit when Cassidy and Banks denied that any definite agreement had been reached. They asserted that De Toth couldn't have rendered his services when the film was contemplated in the summer of 1947, because, at that time, he was working for another studio.

Supposedly, an out-of-court settlement ensued for an unspecified amount.

Paramount's executives were rapidly losing interest in Veronica. With time for only one more picture on her contract, they threw her into another feature, this time a comedy, ironically called *Isn't It Romantic?* The film co-starred Mona Freeman (another actress the studio was billing as "a sensational new discovery"), Mary Hatcher, Billy DeWolfe, Roland Culver, Patric Knowles, and Richard Webb. Adapted from an original story by Jeanette C. Nolan, Norman Z. McLeod was assigned to direct the film with Danny Dare producing. McLeod replaced William Russell, who was the original choice set to direct the picture. The film went through as many title changes as it did directorial. Initially, it was to be called *Father's Day,* and then, *It's Always Spring,* which was the movie's title right up until its release.

Isn't It Romantic? not only turned out to be a disaster at the box office, further damaging Veronica's career, but was just as disastrous while in production. Richard Webb recalls that around the studio the film was being called *Isn't It Ruinous?* because revised script pages were being written right up to the moment of filming.

Veronica protested these conditions one day, in her own funny way. As Webb tells it:

I remember one morning Veronica came to the set and she must have eaten beans before she arrived, because she proceeded to put on quite a show. She had an outrageously funny gaseous attack, cutting farts during every scene. She'd lift her leg before cutting one. The crew cracked up, but Billy DeWolfe, a self-confessed homosexual, pansied around shouting, "Oh, Veronica, stop that. Please s-t-o-p!!!" Veronica didn't listen—she just kept cutting farts to the amusement of her co-workers.

The plot thickened, as did the smell, on the following morning when Mona Freeman and Mary Hatcher decided to join in. Webb continues:

> DeWolfe screamed hysterically, "Oh, come on girls, cut it out. That's enough already . . ." Veronica joined in on the fun, and DeWolfe's order fell on deaf ears as the three of them continued with their show. In the meantime, a group of parochial school children were being taken on tour through the studio just as Veronica, Mona, and Mary began their fart show. The nun leading the pack turned around in disgust and hauled her students out of the studio.

When Veronica wasn't cutting unwanted scents, she was bringing her handiwork to the studio. Between takes, Webb recalled that she would sit down and knit. "Veronica would sit around and knit, and we'd sit around together, like actors do between takes, to talk shop while she'd carry on with her knitting."

Isn't It Romantic?, her final Paramount film, was rated by some critics as "a perfect entertainment vacuum."

In December, Veronica became involved in yet another lawsuit. This time, Cartiers, the New York jewelers, was suing for failure to pay $361 on a bracelet and earrings she had purchased in April of the previous year. No further action was taken, however, when Lake finally forwarded a check to cover the amount.

When Christmas arrived, Veronica was nowhere to be found. She had escaped and only after weeks of searching was she discovered vacationing in Mexico. As a result, no

Christmas celebration was held for the children and an enraged André kept a guarded eye on her from then on. Veronica's mother believes she made the trip to escape from her responsibilities and dilemmas at home.

But Veronica's cat-and-mouse game with André only intensified the rift between them over money. After Christmas, while she resumed filming *Isn't It Romantic?*, André took off once again to some unknown destination to review (he said) possible locations for film properties.

This foolishness continued right through February 1948, when it was determined that Veronica was pregnant again. André was happy over the news, at least temporarily, and demonstrated his support by going on another trip. Veronica has said that Andre wasn't much of a lover, that he viewed her as an object for his sexual pleasure and nothing more.

Shortly after the final take for *Isn't It Romantic?* on April 12, 1948, with Veronica in her third month of pregnancy, André departed to Australia on still another mysterious mission. Insiders believe that André was cheating on Veronica, but it's hard to prove. For the umpteenth time, De Toth left Veronica behind with a desk full of unpaid bills, which kept mounting daily, and her depression to keep her company.

Veronica had very little to feel good about. The only lift was when *Saigon* received its worldwide release on March 12, 1948. The film had some of the magic of the previous Ladd–Lake vehicles, but for the most part, it was a pale imitation. Set in postwar Indochina, Ladd comes across a black marketeer who will pay him ten thousand dollars for a plane ride to steal five hundred thousand dollars out of the territory. Along with his two flying assistants—Luther Adler and Douglas Dick—and Lake, Ladd confiscates the goods but is befriended by the black marketeer in the end. As one critic said, "It's a weak programmer that helped no one's career."

The *The Sainted Sisters* also opened on April 30, 1948. Unfortunately, the film was a lightweight comedy with no direction. Caulfield and Lake portray two 1900s confidence girls on the lam from New York, who find themselves bunked down in a small Maine town near the Canadian border. However, most of the jokes between them are so overblown that little good slapstick results. As the *New York Herald-Tribune's* Howard Barnes wrote: "Miss Lake is properly predatory as the lass who loses her ill-gotten wealth and almost gets it back with interest in the climax. But Caulfield and Lake seem woefully out of place in this period comedy."

With her box-office appeal all but spent, Veronica decided to get even again with André for his loose spending. She took the Navion cross-country to New York without informing him, with her secretary as co-pilot. It felt good to turn on André for once. When she returned home the following week, André was waiting and in a flaming temper. Fuming, he scolded her for risking "the baby" by pulling such an idiotic stunt. She chided back, "What baby is that, André? Do you mean the Navion?" They didn't speak for a week, but Veronica's point was clear.

André was as careless with his plane as he was with Veronica's paychecks. Several weeks later, his license was revoked for piloting the Navion "recklessly and irresponsibly" at Burbank Airport. Afterward, he sold the airplane but found other extravagant ways of spending money, including taking even more extended jaunts around the globe.

During all the commotion, Veronica never heard from her mother. Veronica was primarily responsible for this silence. She thought Constance was out to harm her just like all the rest, despite the fact that Mrs. Keane had come to her aid time and time again. By now, Veronica was afraid not only of André, but everyone. With creditors coming at her from all sides, she isolated herself more and more.

But she couldn't run away from herself. Her career was slipping and her marriage was falling apart. The last and final jolt came when Veronica was hospitalized on October 10, 1948, almost two weeks before her third child was born.

Veronica spent her first few days catching up on correspondence, but during her hospitalization, she received not one phone call or message from her mother. This communication breakdown finally ended when an attorney hired by Mrs. Keane delivered the bad news to Veronica in the hospital. Constance was suing her daughter for failure to uphold weekly payments of $115 a week, based on a 1943 agreement in which she agreed to repay her parents monthly for backing her career. Constance claimed in her suit that Veronica had stopped paying in May 1947, and owed $17,416 in back pay, plus $500 a month for life. There were two reasons for these missed payments: Veronica, who was of aware of the agreement, sometimes paid $50 or $75 rather than the promised $115 weekly, and, André, whose extravagance was leading them into bankruptcy. Nevertheless, André was furious. He called Constance every vile name in the book, Hungarian or otherwise, even though Constance later admitted that she was planning all along to settle out of court.

Veronica didn't have enough energy to tackle the situation. Her pregnancy had left her drained both physically and emotionally. She asked André to leave her alone, but shortly after he left nurses were called to the scene when Veronica became hysterical. She went into such fits that several nurses were required to restrain her. She cried until she fell asleep.

With Veronica in her own little lost world much of the time, Mrs. Keane had hoped that the legal action would wake her daughter to reality. "I just couldn't talk to her anymore. I didn't understand her, and I felt she no longer understood me."

After the suit was filed, a scandalous surge of attacks from both sides was headlined in newspaper stories. In one article, Mrs. Keane claimed that she had recently undergone three major operations, was unable to support herself, and would be dependent upon the charity of others if her daughter didn't come to her assistance. A tiny, graying, bespectacled woman, Constance told the press that the whole situation was disturbing to her, but that it was necessary. "I didn't want to do it. But I had to. I have nothing."

Mrs. Keane spoke to members of the media from the Hollywood home of her friends, Mr. and Mrs. Gregory Ptitsin, where she had stayed for three months. Wearing a faded blue dress, Mrs. Keane was seated on the edge of a chair in her borrowed home and blamed her daughter for negligence. "I had a ten-thousand-dollar-annuity insurance policy and I cashed it to put her over in Hollywood. We got an apartment that perhaps was too luxurious for us, but we had to put up a front for her."

There were few telephone calls from her daughter, Mrs. Keane claimed, and contact between mother and daughter ended with a bracelet on her birthday, a plant at Easter, and a flower arrangement on Mother's Day, 1944. Veronica had "gone Hollywood" and she had come to ignore her family and her background. This was a slight exaggeration on Keane's part and a blatant bid for public sympathy, as proven earlier. Constance was still bitter over the fact that Veronica had not attended the funeral of her stepfather. She had forgotten her family. "It was as if she just dropped from heaven in to Hollywood," Constance said. "How can a daughter forget how her mother fed the family on six dollars a week, while she took dramatic lessons? How can she forget how we gave up cigarettes to save two dollars a week to rent a sewing machine to make her clothes? How can a daughter forget that? I paid for her training and special diction lessons. Nothing was going to stop her from getting her chance. She was my daughter and I wanted her to have it. She was a sweet girl once, but she tossed me out like an old shoe."

To Veronica's comment in the following day's editions that she was supporting everyone, including her mother, Constance retorted, "The money trouble with her has been going on for years. I feel awful that a mother and daughter have such a relationship."

Mrs. Keane was still furious that André De Toth had married Veronica. She scornfully told the press, "I was not invited to her marriage and have never met him. Since then she has never answered my letters, and I have seen Veronica but once. She looked right at me, and passed by. I have lived on promises but if I just had the respect of my daughter, that's all I'd ask—it's all any mother really wants."

In defense, Veronica released the following statement from her hospital bed. It said: "At times, I wasn't financially able to pay [my] mother every week, but as soon as André or I were put back on salary we always paid the backlog. I realize that if she filed the suit it would be a black eye for Hollywood and my children, but I don't want to live my life under a threat."

De Toth had to fight off members of the press daily at the hospital. They kept badgering him for a statement, since he was also named in the suit as a co-defendant for "aiding Miss Lake in evading her responsibility." He wasn't too kind in his remarks. "Veronica's having labor pains already. She's in there sobbing and crying, all on account of this terrible thing. This is a fine thing with which to confront a woman who's about to have a baby. Also a fine way for a grandmother to act." André admitted to the press that the relationship between his wife and Mrs. Keane had been "unfriendly for years" but said he wished his mother-in-law had picked some other time to air her troubles.

The line about Veronica having labor pains was totally untrue, but not unwarranted, as scores of Hollywood columnists, including Hedda Hopper, came to Veronica's rescue and blasted her mother for pulling such a stunt. As Richard Webb, who followed newspaper accounts of the suit, says: "It was very embarrassing for Veronica. One day you'd read what Veronica had to say about her mother, and the next day what her mother had to say about her."

Newspaper headlines sensationalized the situation. Headlines read "MOTHER TELLS WHY SHE SUES VERONICA LAKE," "VERONICA WEEPS AT MOTHER'S SUIT," and "VERONICA'S MONEY JINX SPANS FOUR GENERATIONS." To Hollywood, the mother–daughter feud was the biggest news since Charlie Chaplin's paternity case.

Despite all the bad press, Veronica and André settled out of court. Their attorney, Oliver B. Scwalb, said they didn't have a legal leg to stand on since Mrs. Keane had the legal document, proving Veronica's negligence. After six months of intense deliberation, Constance scored a victory when she was awarded $11,500 to be paid at the rate of $500 a month.

Today, reflecting on the suit, Constance admits that she never received more than the first $500. "De Toth felt I shouldn't have gotten anything. I won the judgment, but I only got back five hundred dollars—that was it. I kept receiving bad checks afterwards that bounced whenever I went to cash them. The court awarded me the money, but they didn't have the money, since De Toth had mishandled it."

Amidst all this legal haggling, the only good news was the arrival on October 16, 1948, of their daughter, Diana, born at 8:30 A.M., and weighing six pounds four ounces. A report from Good Samaritan Hospital described the baby as "doing nicely" and the parents as "very happy."

16
· · · ·

The Falling Star

VERONICA WAS a mental and emotional wreck, bitter over her mother's legal action and still upset with André. It is believed that Veronica suffered a nervous breakdown after these traumatic incidents.

Bedridden, Veronica began drinking excessively at home, far more than she ever had. André accused her of neglecting her responsibilities to him and their children, but Veronica had escaped into the blurred world of the alcoholic.

André put his foot down and suggested that she visit a psychiatrist. She refused, afraid that it would bring further harm to her, that it would only make her suffer more. Veronica even refused to have more than one checkup after each pregnancy with Dr. McBurney, her family physician. She hated the idea of physical examinations, and she was terrified at the idea of having a doctor probe her pysche.

Veronica had grown accustomed to suffering and she was losing touch with the realities of her life. She was now almost completely isolated—no one understood her or her complicated illness. Veronica never had much insight into herself; now her schizophrenia and alcoholism made her a stranger to herself. Unfortunately, André was insensitive to Veronica's needs. He scowled at her every time she mentioned the fact he was spending too much, reminding her that he was the master of the house.

Veronica began accusing André of cheating on her. One night, he came home very late, the fifth time in one week. The next morning, Veronica put André through the third degree. He claimed he had picked up a girl hitchhiking and that he drove her to her intended destination, but that he was detained when she unsuspectingly jumped out of his car, stripped herself naked, ran around his automobile, and then hopped back in, still nude.

Veronica asked, "What did you do next?"

André replied, "I took her home and dropped her off."

Veronica was cleverer than André thought her to be. She had cheated on John several times during their marriage and recognized the signs when André was being dishonest with her. She had always wondered whether his supposed "business trips" included having sex with other women.

But André still knew how to control her. As Helene Nielsen relates: "André may have been all right in his own way, but he was not right for her. He knew what he could do with her and how to control her. He was a terrible man. She'd sit at the table for dinner and he'd say, 'If it wasn't for me, you wouldn't be doing pictures.' He downed her instead of helping her. How would you have liked it if somebody came to you and said, 'Who do you think you are? You were lousy, a nothing, until I picked you up.' If he had been a good man, he would have had insight and feelings."

Usually their arguments would end with Veronica breaking down. As Helene continues: "Veronica would sit there stone-faced as the tears fell down her cheeks, wiping them away in a dignified way, never bringing attention to the fact he had hurt her. It bothered me so much that I would get upset. She'd say to him, 'You're the only one I thought I loved, but somehow I don't really think you love me. If it wasn't for me, you wouldn't be directing pictures.' This was all in a very soft-spoken manner. She hardly ever raised her voice. She was suffering, though, very badly, but tried not showing it."

The financial situation turned so grim that it even affected the children. Elaine was almost seven; Michael, three; and Diana, only two months. The strain of their vanishing finances undoubtedly affected De Toth as well, even though he rarely showed it, but that was no excuse for the way he would discipline Elaine.

Helene Nielsen recalls: "If Elaine didn't eat in a certain time limit, or if she was late for dinner, Andre made her leave the table with no more food for the evening. One time, the nurse found her eating some garbage so he took her and gave her a hair brush-spanking. I sat at the table and was furious, and Veronica sat helplessly and didn't dare try interfering. He was such a bully. I felt helpless as much as Veronica because of my position there, living with them, and knowing the power he had over her. And this happened more than once."

De Toth has been characterized by his peers as militaristic and authoritarian. He'd preen over himself in front of the mirror each morning, glorifying over the body God had given him. In addressing Veronica or the children, he'd bark like a drill sergeant, "Front and center. Front and center." He ran his home as if it was a dictatorship, with Veronica and the children as his subjects.

With her popularity at an all-time nadir, Veronica received the dismal news in November that Paramount was dumping her. She wasn't about to battle the executive board's reason, but her parting words were, "You thankless sons of bitches." Gone was her guaranteed salary of five thousand dollars a week, which had subsidized Andre's sporadic income. After all she had done for the studio, she didn't receive either a farewell party or a thank you.

Everybody close to Lake has various insights as to what led to her downfall. Some say it was due to the fact that the public had begun to identify with her more as a housewife than as an actress. It is also believed that Paramount's brass grew tired of keeping such an explosive and controversial personality under contract. Her public and private exploits tarnished her private and studio image. Others feel she was just a victim of circumstances, with company politics playing to her disadvantage.

As Julie Gibson suggests:

Today's stars are a little smarter. First, they know that their careers are not going to last forever. They know it's a short-lived thing, no matter what. So they take advantage while they can and hire a real good press agent, whom they pay to get the right kind of press. These agents very closely coordinate with these stars what they want their image to be, and see that it is protected and that nothing else gets out. The studio didn't really protect you much in those days, and Veronica became a victim of those circumstances. Her personal life seemed to get caught up in her career. I think that's what did her in. She had all those children to raise and that kind of killed her image right there. She was a mysterious, sexy siren turned into a housewife and suffering marital problems. I believe if her life could have been under control, she could have retained that image and superiority in films. But, unfortunately, she seemed to always pick the wrong men.

Richard Webb, who knew Veronica throughout most of her Hollywood life, explains that public opinion had a lot to do with the studio's decision: "Well, the ratings were down. In those days, they'd pass rating cards out at previews, and once you began to slide, your status was questioned. She wasn't that popular anymore. She no longer had that enigmatic look, she slowed down. She was also misused. The studio began pulling these crappy scripts off the shelves, and began throwing her into them. And, in Veronica's case, the studio used Joan Caulfield as a threat to her stability. She knew why Joan Caulfield was there too." Webb also believes her problems were the direct result of her inability to separate her public and private life. "She was torn between the two, actually," he said.

Teet Carle remembers that members of the studio's publicity department were under the impression that Veronica had lost out to company politics. As he says: "I know that the women in the publicity department were all for Veronica. When she left Paramount, these very same women said, 'She never got what she deserved out of the studio.'"

John Engstead, formerly an art supervisor at Paramount, added: "Poor Veronica, she could have made something of herself; no self-discipline."

Long before, Veronica had shared the same belief with her old friend, Teet Carle: "I remember her telling me once that she always thought she was born with a destiny of becoming one of the greatest personalities in the field of acting. She felt that God had put her on this earth for that reason. I told her that I also had that same feeling when I was young, that the whole world centered around me. She said, 'Teet, maybe you do have a destiny, to help me become the best at what I'm doing. You've always done a lot for me, and I'll never forget you.' "

As with most of her promises, though, Veronica never saw or contacted Carle again. It was her final good-bye.

Job offers were few and far between after news spread throughout Hollywood that Paramount had cut Veronica from its payroll. Somehow, André came up with enough financing to produce one more independent feature through Twentieth Century-Fox, *Slattery's Hurricane,* starring Richard Widmark and Linda Darnell. Unlike her previous films, Veronica was billed third in the film and was given a smaller part than Darnell. The film started production in late November and completed filming in early January. De Toth was hopeful that his earnings from the production would help them pay off their debts.

Slattery's Hurricane was shot on location in Florida, several miles from where Veronica had participated years before in several bathing-beauty contests. The story was based on a study of storm-spotters from the U.S. Weather Bureau, with Veronica portraying an unsympathetic secretary in love with tough guy Widmark. In the film, Widmark plays an ex-naval airman caught up in a dope smuggling scam, who pilots his cargo plane triumphantly through a hurricane to his intended destination. De Toth directed the film and it was a vast improvement over *Ramrod,* containing much more action, which was his forte.

Richard Widmark remembers that Veronica was just as aloof with him as she had been with Alan Ladd. "My memories of Veronica Lake are all good ones. I didn't know her well, for we didn't socialize during the making of *Slattery's*

Hurricane, but professionally, to work with, she was a joy. She was always very polite and extremely professional. She had a wry sense of humor and always seemed happy and enthusiastic during our working days. She was fun to be around."

Widmark also sensed that everything wasn't perfect between Veronica and André. "I gathered that she was having difficulties with her husband, André De Toth, who was directing. But I never knew it—she never gave any indication that she was troubled. I remember that they drove to work in separate matching Cadillacs. That did seem a bit much."

As with *Ramrod,* the harmony between De Toth and the co-workers also became strained. According to Widmark, Twentieth Century-Fox president, Daryl Zanuck, was involved too. "The picture was a bad one, and Zanuck had us do extensive added scenes and retakes three different times. He finally flipped the movie over and *started* the thing with the end. But Veronica took it all in stride—totally unperturbed. The script was always in a turmoil. De Toth was working on it with a writer named A. I. Bezzarides and he would hand us new pages to shoot practically every morning. I finally blew up at De Toth and Veronica just stood by smiling. Maybe she enjoyed watching me confront her husband. I don't know."

Slattery's Hurricane premiered on a navy aircraft carrier, the U.S.S. *Constitution,* several days before mainland audiences viewed the film at the Loew's Chinese Theater on August 9, 1949. The film pleased the critics and made De Toth just enough to pay off most of his debts. Critical notices mostly raved over the film's special effects, including the creation of the realistic storm sequences involving the flight of Widmark's plane.

By December 1949, however, André and Veronica

were near bankruptcy, temporarily averted by the profits from *Slattery's Hurricane*. They were able to afford a trip back to New York with Veronica's old friend, Howard Hughes.

Hughes invited them on TWA's inauguration of coast-to-coast service. The flight took off on February 15, 1950, with Hughes at the controls. Also on board was a celebrated group of movie stars, including Cary Grant, Virginia Mayo, Walter Pidgeon, Mr. and Mrs. William Powell, Jack Carson, Jack Warner, Linda Darnell, Edward G. Robinson, Tyrone and Annabella Powers, Janet Blair, Paulette Goddard, Myrna Loy, Frank Morgan, David Selznick, and Randolph Scott and his wife, Gene Tierney. An uninvited guest who Veronica remembered quite well also hopped aboard —Constance Moore, who kept her distance from Lake.

Veronica's trip back East was like a homecoming. All was upbeat and gay until the last night in town when André took Veronica to the famed watering hole, the Stork Club. Their table was right next to Walter Winchell's, who inquired about Veronica's career and André's plans for his wife. Their chat was cordial, with Andre acting like a politician, offering Winchell several rounds of drinks in the hopes that he would give Veronica a good write-up. It was the most fun she had had in quite some time.

Unfortunately, as they said goodnight to the Stork's owner, Sherman Billingsley, a young man reached out from the bar to touch Lake's golden hair. He was a fan in his early twenties, and the gesture seemed perfectly harmless. Not to André. It was as if someone was trying to steal the golden fleece. De Toth whirled around and started punching the man, four or five times, according to witnesses, before an army major pulled them apart.

The fan never raised a finger. André's punches all hit their marks and he was still enraged. The young man's face was bloodied and he held his hands over his head in pain, slumping over the bar. The major, grabbing André by the shirt collar, growled, "I ought to belt you right in the mouth."

"Get your hands off me," André barked right back.

The major was so sympathetic with the young lad that he decided to take matters into his own hands. He pushed back at André and shoved him outside, challenging him to a match right on the sidewalk, until Billingsley intervened. Fortunately, no punches were thrown. But De Toth's reputation and credit at the Stork Club were not improved. Holding De Toth and ordering the major back in the club, Billingsley remarked, "That was a pretty poor stunt, André."

Obsessed, De Toth said, "I'm not sorry. I don't want anyone touching her."

"Then stay out of here forever," Billingsley said.

This stormy episode made all the major newspapers and wire services across the country. It revealed De Toth's true personality but also tarnished Veronica's already questionable image. In the public's mind, De Toth was "a kook" for belting a fan over something as trivial as touching her hair. On February 19, 1950, newspaper headlines said it all: "VERONICA LAKE'S HAIR BLAMED IN FISTICUFFS."

When asked to comment on the encounter, André explained: "We were preparing to leave the club. As we walked through the bar, a man reached out for her hair. I guess I lost my temper. I let out a swing. Maybe once, maybe twice. I think I hit him in the face, but I don't remember him going down. After the confusion died down, Miss Lake and I left. I don't know the man's name. I wish it hadn't happened at all."

Surprisingly, the unnamed man didn't file charges of assault against De Toth. Maybe he was a true fan.

Afterward, Veronica and André returned to the Chatsworth ranch. She began losing her patience with him, her personal frustration compounded by the fact she wasn't being offered any new movie roles. Instead, she kept receiving calls from creditors over past-due bills. Veronica continued to rely on alcohol for solace.

Then, in early April, with money worries heightening, André took Veronica on a trip to Mexico to attend a spring festival. While vacationing in this sungoers' haven, it was reported in the *Los Angeles Times* that Veronica and André were sinking into deeper financial woes. According to the article, Veronica had to sell her sleek 1949 Cadillac convertible at a sheriff's auction on March 9 to satisfy the dealer's balance. It was bought by Chet Huntley, then a radio news commentator for NBC. Her big, rambling home on its secluded hilltop in Chatsworth was also in question. Holders of the first deed were considering taking it over, filing a notice of default.

Reached in Mexico to comment on this, De Toth told members of the press that he was searching for some eleventh-hour solution. Veronica tried finding work on her own. In the late spring, she flew to New York to pawn some jewelry and guest-star on Milton Berle's *Texaco Star Theater* on NBC. The money was pretty good considering television was still in its infancy (she received $2,500, but it was the exposure she needed the most). According to Eddie LeRoy, Berle's faithful sidekick, Miltie knew that Veronica was suffering and tried to help. "Milton tried to keep her spirits high. He always helped those who needed help, and sensed that Veronica was having troubles, which was another reason why he had her on the show. To show how much he cared, Milton had a large flower arrangement delivered after the show, which practically filled her dressing room."

With such moral support, Veronica continued to play the gamut of roles on television. In October, she made an appearance on *Shadow of the Heart,* a one-hour dramatic presentation by CBS. This was followed by a guest-starring role as the hostess on Sid Caesar's *Your Show of Shows.* Lake and Caesar performed one skit together, "We Love Life," and Veronica was the hit of the evening. To earn a few more dollars, Veronica starred again as a witch, her first such role since *I Married a Witch,* in "Beware of This Woman," an episode of *Lights Out.*

During these performances, Veronica was very much the lady. She didn't make waves or harsh demands. She didn't show up drunk. Down to her last dollar, she was fully cooperative in this last-ditch effort to save herself and André. With these earnings, she and André were able to achieve a shaky financial equilibrium. She also pawned her personal possessions that no longer had any sentimental value to her.

Following the Caesar show, using some of Veronica's hard-earned money, André went on another business excursion, this time to London to seek potential film properties. Veronica was, to say the least, irritated with her husband's frequent departures in times of monetary stress, but she wasn't strong enough to stop him. With André gone, Veronica took her career into her own hands for once and accepted an offer to star in a low-budget Mexican film, *Stronghold.* Later, she admitted, "It was a dog but the pay was decent." Lake starred opposite Zachary Scott and Artuoro De Cordova. The film took a little less than two months to shoot.

It was only upon her return to the Chatsworth ranch that André first learned about her whereabouts. Nobody knew that she was in Mexico, not even the hired help, since she didn't leave word with anybody—not even Helene. De

Toth came back from London to an empty house and at first wondered if she had been kidnapped. He was wild when he found out that she had "cheapened herself" by starring in such a grade-B production. He told Veronica that he had been saving "great things for her." But she now knew better than to believe him.

All during their seven-year marriage, André's promises were about as good as the paper on which they were written. Her marital woes heightened, however, when he accused her of fooling around with one of the Mexican film stars. That was the last straw, and as far as Veronica was concerned, the distance between them had opened for the last time.

In April 1951, Veronica and André filed voluntary petitions of bankruptcy in U.S. Court, listing debts of $156,-573.91 and assets of $168,050. The principal assets listed were their ranch home in Chatsworth, which they valued at $120,000, and $45,000 that Veronica claimed was owed to her from her performance in *Stronghold*. The petition also itemized almost one hundred creditors with claims varying from a few dollars to several hundred dollars.

The Chatsworth ranch, which the bankruptcy petition stated had two encumberances totaling $36,900 against it, was seized by a collector of internal revenue for unpaid income taxes of approximately $63,000. The ranch was to be put up for sale at public auction to satisfy the tax bill. In addition to unpaid income taxes, the petition in bankruptcy noted that the state of California had a tax lien of $13,000 against the Chatsworth ranch and that unpaid Los Angeles county and municipal taxes tallied another $5,000, the equivalent of Veronica's former weekly salary at Paramount.

Veronica and André moved to a smaller, secluded, home on 6630 Jamen Avenue in Reseda. Helene Nielsen was asked to move out. Recalling the incident, Nielsen said recently: "André told her to make me leave. She came to me and said, 'Helene, I love you and want you here.' She never talked directly, she was very soft-spoken, with her eyes down. She felt badly to have to tell me. But she said, 'André wants you to leave.' I didn't know where the hell I was going, but I left."

In a statement to the press, the De Toths blamed the government's seizure of their home on their present financial difficulties. As André said: "When the government seized our home all our creditors came down on us at once. Some of the bills were not even due. We had money coming and could have paid the bills if we had had time." So he claimed, anyway.

The auction of the Chatsworth ranch was scheduled for May 8, 1951, at which time fifty potential buyers viewed the property. Minimum bid was $65,000. But there were no takers. In fact, no bids were made at all.

Christopher Gilbert, field division chief for the Bureau of Internal Revenue, served as the auctioneer and when he described the property it took the better part of an hour. Among the twenty-four acre estate, there were three bedrooms, three baths, stables for five horses, groom's quarters, and several outbuildings.

With creditors pawing for their money, the bankruptcy court reevaluated the De Toth's assets and split them up among the various merchants. Some of the unpaid bills included orchid corsages from André to Veronica. Much of the pending $63,000 tax debt was paid off when Lake received her back salary from *Stronghold,* and with the eventual sale of the Chatsworth ranch.

Veronica was ready for a new lease on life—which didn't include André. In June 1951, following months of acrimonious discussion, Veronica filed for separation from her husband of almost eight years, citing no compelling reason for the action, just that their relationship had finally been strained.

Following the separation, Veronica rejected offers to star in assorted low-budget films. Her reason: "I really didn't want to go back through the grind of playing sexy sirens in grade-B thrillers all for the silk purses of the studio management." Instead, putting her three children in the temporary custody of a governess, Veronica bade farewell to Hollywood permanently, packing her bags and moving to New York. It was in Manhattan that she hoped to heal all wounds and start life anew.

17

. . . .

Life on Stage

Nᴇᴡ ʏᴏʀᴋ ᴡᴀs ʜᴏᴍᴇ as far as she was concerned, and she moved into a comfortable brownstone in Greenwich Village. She was relieved to have André out of her life, and was ready to revitalize her career. Television presented the first outlet for her to explore thanks to her recent success in this new entertainment medium.

During the first three months of living in New York, she appeared on nine television shows. Veronica found her appearances on the tube both challenging and lucrative, paying two thousand five hundred dollars per performance. As with radio, Veronica disliked the idea of performing in front of a live audience. It still frightened her to death, even though money talked.

This natural fear would follow her when she pursued a third career in the legitimate theater. She discovered that the stage was more demanding than the movie set and required more rehearsals than with live television. With three children to raise, Veronica's stage work was somewhat prohibitive at first. After she settled in New York, she sent for the children, but she found little time to be with them. How would she travel on the road with three children to raise? She solved this in a number of ways. Sometimes she'd take them with her on tour, which wasn't often, or ship them back to André for safekeeping, even though the children reportedly hated staying with him. On other occasions, Veronica's friends and neighbors pitched in to babysit.

Veronica admitted that her children might have had fewer problems later in life if she had been able to be with them more. According to Veronica's mother, Elaine's children by her first marriage were taken into custody by the city's welfare department because of her inability to provide them with a proper home. Michael had been a problem child from the day he was born. As a teenager, he was constantly in jail for stealing cars and for other criminal acts. Diana was the only one of the three who grew up to lead a somewhat normal life.

Veronica's first stage hit was *Voice of the Turtle*. It opened in late spring at a theater-in-the-round in Atlanta, Georgia. The program was billed as her first stage appearance as the female lead. On opening night, Veronica's performance drew a packed house and a legion of critics. Upon her first entrance she received a standing ovation and flashbulbs from theatergoers' cameras exploded to record this historic event.

Physically, Veronica appeared much older than her age. She was only thirty-one, but alcoholism had bloated her face and thickened her body. Her weight was hovering at one hundred and ten, nearly twenty pounds overweight.

Her honey-colored hair glistened in the stage's lights, but gone was the peekaboo look, replaced by a thinning version with her long tresses dangling on the sides of her face.

The show had its drawbacks. Carl Betz, her co-star, was reportedly a very egocentric performer. His appearance was so important to him that on opening night he missed his first cue. Furious, Veronica excused herself in front of the audience and scurried backstage to Betz's dressing room. There he was daintily combing each strand of hair in place and admiring himself in front of the mirror. Veronica exploded, "Get your pretty ass out here."

"I'm not ready," Betz flatly retorted.

Growling even louder, Veronica said, "Ready or not, you have an obligation to perform. Now get out there."

Betz finally obliged, but afterward he complained to the show's director about Veronica, refusing to work with "such a has-been actress." Fortunately, the director was able to smooth out Betz's ruffled feathers, and he showed more patience with Lake as the show continued. In due time, in fact, Veronica and Betz were to be seen buddying around with each other after work, often drinking together at a local tavern.

It was around this time that Veronica vented her feelings about what it was like working on stage: "It was something entirely different for me. I never had a voice. Or at least I've never been called upon to use it in the movies or it wasn't properly developed. Now it appears that some of my theater work will be with the traditional proscenium, so I'll have to work on a new pitch." Veronica also commented that she found the theater to be a more healthful medium than the movies. The hours allowed her plenty of time for sleeping in the mornings, if she liked, and to get outdoors in the afternoons. In Hollywood, the usual schedule was from dawn-to-dusk daily, and there was also the big disadvantage of being unable to spend much time with the children, even though that was never much of a priority with her.

Lake also found that theater work had something else going for it—first-hand appreciation. "When the people applaud, I just love it, even though their enthusiasm does bring out all the ham in me." Veronica was also happy to change her peekaboo coiffure for a simpler one.

Living in New York also had its advantages. She was able to lead a much more private life. She said: "I found myself being something more real than a movie star. Everyone else when they have a job start work at one hour and finish at another, but every Miss Glamour Puss is expected to work at it twenty-four hours a day, and no one can exist like that."

Defending her stage work, she later said: "I loved every minute of it. Gone was the plush facade of Hollywood. Replacing it was honesty, raw and meaningful vitality, that shone bright in the murky memories of California and its film factory."

After a Birmingham engagement, *Voice of the Turtle* returned for one last encore performance in Atlanta before closing its doors. Afterward, Veronica was cast in another touring show, *The Curtain Rises.* It was described as "a slipshod operation" at best—and for good reason. In Fayetteville, New York, when the prop men walked out, Veronica and several other actors had to help finish painting the sets. At Matunuck-by-the-Sea, Rhode Island, the curtain collapsed in the middle of the performance. Then, in Watkins Glen, New York, there was a dispute with the salaried ticket-selling personnel, and Lake was eventually forced to answer phones and sell tickets right up to curtain time.

Veronica behaved herself most of the time. Many of the producers and directors had heard about her explosive personality, but, to their utter amazement, there were very few occasions when she instigated any type of ruckus. She was so worn out emotionally that she had lost most of her spunk. She just wanted to survive.

After *The Curtain Rises* closed, Veronica took about two months off to relax before hunting for another show. What turned up in the interim was not exactly a natural for her: *Peter Pan.* Her children were incredulous about the role and said they'd laugh if they saw their mother wearing tights, a vest, and a pixie haircut.

Since Peter Pan represented youthful exuberance, Veronica whipped herself back into shape by temporarily cutting off the booze and dieting on a half-pound of grapes each morning, followed by calisthenics. She also took weekly fencing lessons to help tone her legs, stomach, and arm muscles. Proclaiming herself "tight and energetic," Veronica opened the show to an enthusiastic throng on October 10, 1951, at the Lyric Theatre in Baltimore, Maryland, before the production moved to New York. According to *Variety,* Veronica gave "a boyish quality and engaging matter-of-fact reading to the whimsical lead character that projects to an entire audience, young and old." In this version of the famous J. M. Barrie play, music and lyrics were written by Leonard Bernstein; Frank Corsaro directed; and Lawrence Tibbets was cast as the nefarious Captain Hook.

Theatergoers were amazed to discover how gracefully Veronica moved across the stage as Peter Pan, especially in light of rumors that had her temper interfering with the show.

The classic story stems from opening night. A major mishap occurred with the rigging that enabled Veronica to fly. One of the production's three assistants, Peter Foy, was placed in charge of operating the rig of wires, pulleys, ropes, and specially made harnesses that enabled the actors to be airborne. The harnesses were concealed under the costumes of the actors. Foy would pull on hemp ropes attached to thirty-five-foot steel cables to make the players take off.

In the middle of opening night, everything was going along just fine until it was time for the three other characters and Veronica to fly. Foy attached the wrong cable to Lake's harness. As a result, she sailed across the stage uncontrollably, tangling wires with the other actors, and crashing into the mast of a prop ship on stage, hanging on until the curtain was closed. Following this near-catastrophe, it was reported that Veronica had a few choice words with Foy on the art of flying.

Even though *Peter Pan* was well received critically, it wasn't a box-office success. The show played in New York and in Los Angeles, but failed to conjure up the type of business the promoters were hoping for. As a result, *Peter Pan* stopped touring at the end of January.

Veronica didn't want to leave the show. Afterward, she said that depression crept in and that she languished for lack of work. She never realized how much she had enjoyed stage work until it was over. The theater had been good for her ego and had helped restore her self-esteem. But she became even more depressed when a feature she had made two years earlier was finally released.

Stronghold debuted to film audiences on January 31, 1952, at the Orpheum, Ritz, and Vogue theatres in Hollywood. Released by Lippert Pictures, the film was set in the 1850s and cast Veronica as a wealthy silver mine owner who gets caught up in a Mexican revolution. The film was made in both English and Spanish versions and was placed on the double-bill kiddie markets in America. As *Variety* charitably noted: "Miss Lake does the best she can." *Hollywood Re-*

porter was in agreement with most critics when it complained that the film had "few stirring scenes" and "a thin plot."

The film's release couldn't have been more ill-timed. Veronica was just beginning to establish new credibility in the field of legitimate theater and didn't need a flop, which *Stronghold* was. It lasted in theaters for only one week.

By this time, Veronica had turned to the bottle again, though she didn't let her drinking interfere with her work on stage as much as she had in Hollywood. There were no reports of her reeling to rehearsals each day from a hard night's drinking.

Although drinking advanced her depression, her career was given a much-needed boost when she landed a series of jobs in stock company productions, beginning with *The Gramercy Ghost of Matunuck*. But her work in that production was short-lived when she contracted a severe virus.

Rebounding from her ill-health, Lake next starred in *I Am a Camera* during the summer of 1952 on the New England coast. This was followed by another stage revue, *Cat on a Hot Tin Roof*, which accentuated her constant battles with her health. During one rehearsal, she fell off the stage and landed in the orchestra pit. She sustained a badly sprained ankle with torn ligaments and tendons. A local physician fixed up the leg in a walking cast and gave her permission to perform, provided she received three shots of novocain in the ankle before each show. The cast was concealed under her petticoat.

Once *Cat on a Hot Tin Roof* concluded its brief run, Veronica hoped to return to Broadway in a romantic comedy entitled *Masquerade*. The play was set in present-day Rome with Veronica portraying the role of a street gamin. The show had played a warmup engagement in Springfield,

Massachusetts, but poor reviews dashed all hopes of playing on Broadway and *Masquerade* limped into Philadelphia on April 16, 1953. *Variety*'s assessment was brief: "Miss Lake is unable to extract much sense from the role of the virtuous waif." Much to Veronica's own chagrin, the show folded in Philadelphia and her dream of playing on Broadway was left unfulfilled.

Even though Veronica kept switching from one show to another, her appeal with the press hadn't diminished. She was still frequently interviewed for magazine and newspaper features. The questioning focused on her two disastrous marriages and her walking out on Hollywood. In answer to whether she planned to resume a movie career, she replied, "I'm not mad at Hollywood or show business and I'm not complaining. I should and I do appreciate the good fortune I found. Certainly the people I worked with, more often than not, were wonderful to me. I simply lost my personal identity and wanted to get it back."

By the spring of 1954, Veronica was seen cavorting with Joe McCarthy, not the politician, but the son of famous music publisher, Joseph McCarthy, Sr. Little Joe, a graduate of Juilliard University, was also in the music publishing field as a songwriter. McCarthy met Veronica when his good friend and fellow songwriter, Austin "Ginger" Johnson, introduced them to each other. It was instant love, the first time for Veronica.

She found that she and Joe could talk on a variety of subjects openly and comfortably. What wasn't apparent at first, however, was Joe's complete sense of failure, the result of living in the shadow of his great father. Everybody expected him to attain the same type of prominence as Joe McCarthy, Sr. So he was also looking for an identity. Veronica later observed that under his mask hostility boiled. She felt that even though he was usually open, he sometimes held things back. Otherwise, Joe was very compassionate and lavished her with constant admiration.

Joe and Veronica also shared one other bond of interest: they both loved to drink. During their courtship, they often went "pub-crawling," as Veronica called it, coming back soused to her apartment. Lake never realized that Joe was more of a drinking buddy than a potential husband.

If she had only realized this before they were married on August 28, 1955, in Traverse City, Michigan, another personal hardship might have been avoided. Veronica was appearing locally in *Affairs of State,* when Joe popped the question. The couple were married on the day of the show's final performance. McCarthy was four years younger than Veronica: he was thirty-two and she was thirty-six.

Joe and Veronica moved to another brownstone on Ninth Street in Greenwich Village, where McCarthy received his first taste of fatherhood. He certainly had his hands full with Elaine, Michael, and Diana, although it was Michael who presented most of the trouble. Elaine married a local businessman named Maynard Berger, making Joe's job easier. During the next few years, they would make Veronica a grandmother three times.

However, Michael must have had a demon inside of him. He was always getting into trouble. The McCarthy's apartment featured a luscious willowy tree in the front yard that bristled up against the living room window. The tree became Michael's favorite playground. He always avoided the front doorway and made his entrance sliding down one of the tree's branches through the open living room window. Half the time he popped in unexpectedly when Veronica either had guests or she was alone. It drove Veronica and Joe crazy. Joe was incapable of expressing anger or other emotions consistently but, like Veronica, he'd blow his stack on occasion. He also had zero experience at raising children. He didn't like Veronica's traveling all the time, and felt it was her duty to take care of Michael and Diana. The real test came when Veronica won a part in *The Little Hut,* which opened in Detroit, Michigan, shortly after their marriage. It kept her on the road for three months of the original ten-month tour, but was cancelled when Veronica collapsed one night from stage exhaustion. It was then that Joe requested that she stop overworking herself.

But Veronica was a hungry woman. She wanted to make up for the many times André had kept her on a leash. Even though marriage was a full-time commitment, this time around she wanted to have some freedom as well.

Joe gave up when their home life turned sour. Veronica and he were constantly at each other's throats, griping and bitching over the smallest of things. One day, Veronica merely asked to use the bedroom phone. Joe got so mad that he refused, kicking her in the back and knocking her to the floor. Getting up slowly, Lake thought her back had been broken and hobbled out to the living room. But Joe wasn't through. He kept up his verbal war with Veronica until Michael, with a blood-curdling grin on his face, dashed out of the kitchen brandishing a butcher knife.

Michael chased Joe out of the apartment and into the streets of the Village. Once he lost Michael, Joe returned to the apartment in hopes of patching up his differences with Veronica. Waiting for him in the tree, Michael jumped down in front of his stepfather and held the knife to Joe's throat. Another chase resulted, but this time, Veronica called the police and asked them to issue a warrant against Joe for simple assault. Michael was fourteen years old at the time, and, as Veronica once said, he usually defended her in the most unorthodox ways.

Joe was placed in jail with bail set at five hundred dollars. Veronica dropped the assault charges and her husband was released, but she was still mad enough about the entire incident to file for a separation in March 1959.

Veronica later admitted that during her three-and-a-half-year marriage to Joe, they were separated half of the time. She confessed in court that her only moments of marital compatibility with Joe were when they went on drunken sprees together. In fact, many of her fondest memories of the time with McCarthy were blocked by her heavy drinking, leaving them mostly one big blur. Joe countersued for separation, with Veronica demanding thirteen thousand dollars alimony a year. The courts failed to see why she deserved such lucrative compensation and awarded her sixty-four dollars a week.

It was this third divorce that proved to be her ultimate undoing. She was evicted from her Ninth Street apartment when she fell behind on her monthly rent.

Afterward, Veronica tried to save face when she made a rare television appearance on *The Eddie Cantor Comedy Theatre*. Syndicated to television in the spring, Lake appeared in the comedy episode, "A Hunting We Will Go," with Craig Stevens. This appearance would be followed by almost three years of professional inactivity. With no stable income other than her alimony, Veronica found she had nothing left except drinking. For long periods of time she drank for oblivion—to forget the past and soften the present. Sometimes, however, when she had not been boozing too heavily, she would have a disconcerting flash of clarity. At those times she wondered where else to turn.

18

· · · ·

Rediscovered

VERONICA HAD DROPPED to the lowest ebb of her life. She had taken such a long hiatus from acting that some producers wondered whether she was dead or alive. Veronica would have preferred to be the former.

After the split with Joe, Veronica rented a small apartment in the Greenwich Village area, but not as plush as her previous residence. She paid a year's rent in advance out of money she had saved from her summer stock earnings. She also came up with enough cash to enroll Michael in Grove School, a military boarding school in Connecticut. Ironically, Veronica was pulling the same act her mother had in sending her to the Villa Maria Convent School. Michael, now seventeen, also needed someone with a firm hand to provide him with 'round the clock tutelage. Veronica then lost Diana to André, who took her along with him to Switzerland, where she attended private school. Thus, with Elaine married, Veronica was finally alone and free—no more household worries except for herself.

Before Michael began his first semester, Veronica was invited by one of Michael's older friends, Charles, to spend the Labor Day weekend at Forest Hills, where the annual tennis competition was slated. After the matches, Charles and Veronica were invited to have drinks and dinner at another friend's house. Later that evening, when Charles and Veronica were dancing, Charles tried spinning her around. When Charles, who weighed two hundred and forty pounds, accidentally tripped and fell on Veronica's foot, it broke like a matchstick.

She was immediately rushed to Queens Hospital where she was put in a cast. In and out of hospitals for the next eight months, Veronica spent three of them with a traction cast up to her hip. This medical fiasco alone drained four thousand dollars out of her savings, money she needed to survive.

During her recuperation, she managed to hobble around but the ankle was slow to heal. Her financial plight was such that she didn't even have one cent for groceries or to pay the electric bills. She wouldn't have made it if it hadn't been for several generous friends, including Nat Perlow.

Perlow, an editor for the *New York Police Gazette*, was her primary savior. Nat was a happy-go-lucky individual who always gave Veronica, besides his usual cheerfulness, bags of groceries and money for support. Nat became so close to Veronica, in fact, that if she hadn't been so down on marriage she probably would have married him. He maintained his good friendship from afar, providing Veronica with a much-needed boost at a time when it was a matter of survival.

Men like Perlow were important to Veronica, because, as Helene Nielson points out, "I think she realized what few friends she had. Coping with that image was not easy. She needed others to help her get over her many hurts."

In early 1961, approximately a year and a half after her accident, Veronica's ankle had practically healed. She needed a cane for support, and she hadn't worked in all this time. Bills kept piling up higher and higher, and sometimes she'd miss her rent for three months in a row. Her cue for payment was a knock on her door by the landlord, who would give her twenty-four hours to scrape up the necessary back rent, or be evicted.

With her ankle healed, she finally resumed her search for work in legitimate theater and elsewhere. But nobody was interested. She had been away from acting too long—nearly six years. Producers at her auditions concluded that she was stale and had lost her zing.

She found temporary employment in a factory downtown where she pasted felt flowers on lingerie hangers. It's hard to imagine the former movie star working in a minimum-wage job.

Then, the break she had been waiting for arrived. Veronica left her job in the factory to become a cocktail waitress in the Martha Washington Hotel on East 29th Street. At night, she was employed in the Colonnade Room cocktail lounge and during the day she slept in a hotel room that she rented for seven dollars a day. According to newspaper reports at the time, Veronica was earning between twenty to thirty-five dollars a day in tips in her part-time position.

Despite what others thought, Veronica claimed to really enjoy her job. She took great pleasure in mingling with the customers, from merchant marines to local prostitutes to down-on-their-luck businessmen to alcoholics. These were her kind of people. The bar regulars called her Connie, Ronni, and sometimes, Veronica. But none of them knew that she was Veronica Lake. To them, she was just Veronica the barmaid.

Helene Nielsen fully understood why her cousin enjoyed her new position. In an interview, she said: "I think that being a bar hostess, she knew that not too much was expected of her. She was really down on her luck, and that dragged her down. But working with people who had a few dollars to spend and time to talk must have made her feel wanted."

Whatever the reason, on March 22, 1962, newspapers had a field day when a *New York Post* article revealed that Lake had been rediscovered working as a barmaid. With this deluge of press attention, queries and job offers poured in from the entertainment world, all urging her to make a comeback. There were offers of up to fifteen thousand dollars for an engagement in Las Vegas, a part in an off-Broadway play, a role in a Twentieth Century-Fox movie, and a chance to appear on television in *Naked City*. She refused all of them.

Veronica was caught off-guard by this sudden renewed interest. She had become accustomed to living in obscurity. When the *Post* story broke, reporters were constantly fighting to interview her for their own newspapers. Veronica consented but under the condition that there be absolutely "no pictures" taken of her. As one reporter chronicled: "The famous locks of hair which hung flirtatiously across her face, covering one eye, now are nothing more than a fading memory. Most of the time she wears her hair pulled tightly back." Ironically, the reporter also noted that Veronica played women in her films who were usually down on their luck. But Veronica told reporters, "I'm not destitute."

Yet she scoffed at the idea of a comeback. From time to time, producers and other members of the entertainment business would drop in to discuss an offer. One time, a man sat down at the booth and asked her if she'd be interested in a part in a play. Veronica quickly changed the subject. On another occasion, a local producer came in to pitch a movie proposal to her. She talked to him for a few minutes, then turned away. Fans sent her cards and letters, with money enclosed, from places as far away as Japan, Sweden, and Australia, but her pride made her refuse these contributions; she sent them all back.

Frankly, Veronica was embarrassed by the attention. She preferred the anonymity and tranquility her new life style offered. She had moved to New York to escape from being a celebrity. But now her true identity was no longer a secret to the bar patrons. Sometimes her movies would be shown locally and everyone in the bar would shove aside their drinks to watch her on the tavern's television set. *The Blue Dahlia* or *Sullivan's Travels* were often shown separately, or as part of a week-long festival.

During Veronica's four-month tenure at the Martha Washington she met someone very special. His name was Andy Elickson and he was a merchant seaman who often drank with his shipmates at the Colonnade Room.

One night, when Elickson and his three partners got sloshed, the bar's manager ordered Veronica to kick them out. She went over and politely warned them to quiet down or suffer the consequences. Andy was the rugged leader of the bunch. He was strong, heavy set and muscular, with a Wallace Beery smile. His blond hair had tinges of gray and his Norwegian accent was still evident. He was also a huggable-looking fellow, built like an oversized teddy bear, standing six feet tall and weighing two hundred and forty pounds. That didn't change Veronica's job responsibilities, however. When Elickson's party got too loud, she physically grabbed them one by one and tossed them out of the bar. Andy returned at 2 A.M., alone and subdued. This time, he behaved himself and promised Veronica that there would be "no more rough stuff." Andy asked Veronica out to an all-night restaurant for coffee and clams afterward. Impressed by his softness, she accepted.

Andy was married, but he had been separated for five years. There was something different about Andy. He wasn't as demanding as her three previous husbands, but easy-going and a pleasure to be with. Gradually, their nights together increased and by April 1962, Veronica had quit her job at the Colonnade Room to be with Andy. She spent every possible moment with him, and, between his frequent trips, she lived with him.

During this time, Andy still insisted that he had never heard her name before. He had no idea she was the aging actress who made male filmgoers during the 1940s lust for her body. He liked her just the way she was. In remembering their relationship, Veronica once described Andy as "rough within bounds, serious when making love, but playful." Most of all, however, they just enjoyed each other's company.

Several months later, Andy finally figured out who Veronica was. He had been talking with some fellows down at the dock and he said to her afterward, "You're the one with the hair, aren't you?" It didn't change his feeling about her one iota. Instead, he continued as if there was nothing different about her. They would lie together every evening in bed, drinking, smoking, making love, until they fell asleep.

In time, however, no amount of lovemaking could substitute for the bare essentials of survival. It wasn't fair to mooch off Andy, and, besides, he was sometimes gone for months at a time.

Luck, for once, turned in her favor when WJZ-TV, a Baltimore station, advertised an opening for a hostess to introduce and talk about films on its Saturday night film program, *Festival of Stars*. A friend named Jeff Sparks encouraged Veronica to apply, and she won the job instantly.

The pay was adequate and enabled Veronica to rent a plush apartment on New York's East Side. She commuted to Baltimore on weekends to tape the show and became more comfortable with each broadcast. The station owned rights to one of her films, *I Married a Witch*. One night, with that film as the main attraction, her off-mike comment during the broadcast was "I wonder whatever happened to that broad?" Fans let her know, sparking a flood of fan mail. The show's ratings soared and the program proved to be quite successful for the station.

In January 1963, Veronica returned for another season of hosting the Baltimore TV program. She also rejoined Andy Elickson, who was back from a voyage to India. Her relationship with Elickson was now mostly platonic, with occasional bursts of passion. She was content with her new life with Andy, but missed his moral support when traveling kept him away often. By early summer he had shipped off once again for Tampa Bay and other ports along the eastern seaboard. Sometimes Veronica would meet him at these destinations, flying down for the weekend to be with him.

Unlike the past few months, however, Veronica was itching to work in theater again. In August 1963, she received her chance. Arthur Whitlow, who was producing a revival of *Best Foot Forward,* called to offer her the lead role in the show. She was to replace Paula Wayne, who had quit the show. Lake accepted and she portrayed the character of Gale Joy, a fading movie queen, whose career parallelled Veronica's own.

Following week-long rehearsals, the show reopened

on August 29, 1963, at Stage 73 in New York. The appreciative audience gave Veronica a standing ovation. Lake said she "cried like a baby." It was the greatest experience of her stage life. She told reporters before the premiere: "I'm really playing a burlesque of myself, of Veronica Lake. But I didn't mind because I like to clown and how else can you explain clowning."

Veronica also admitted that she was suffering from opening night jitters. "I was scared silly. But it was great. Damn, it's great to be back. I think in this show, people will be able to see what I can do."

Critics agreed, and columnists predicted that the show would spur a long-awaited comeback. But it never did. Veronica did not appear on a stage again until many years later.

Her relationship with Andy was also ending. He was at sea so much of the time that she was lucky if she got to see him a couple times out of the year. She didn't hear from him next until April 1965, two years later, when he sent a telegram from San Francisco, asking her to join him. Andy was preparing for another foreign tour, this time to Vietnam. Veronica loved Andy—but not enough to marry him.

Their time together in San Francisco was very short. Andy left the following morning on what was originally scheduled as a three-month journey. Instead, it stretched to eight months. Veronica didn't see Andy again until one year later in Galveston. The man who greeted her was not the same man who had left. Andy had been reduced from a 240-pound strongman to a 160-pound shell of his former self. His body was frail and thin, and Veronica felt the loss of strength when he hugged her. Andy jokingly attributed it to a diet of Vietnamese food. Besides, he said, "I needed to lose the weight anyway." Andy was a weak and sick man, but how sick he didn't know. When she stayed with him in

New York, Veronica noticed that he deteriorated each day.

Andy took another short trip in April, but after that retreated to his New York hotel and to the bottle. He was in much more pain than before. His legs were bloated and his kidneys ached.

Veronica also took refuge in the bottle. Watching Andy slowly waste away to skin and bones was too much to bear. She got herself drunk practically every night at her old stomping grounds, the Colonnade Room.

Her inebriated ways were given a good deal of press attention when one night she was discovered outside a local Catholic church. She wasn't able to face Andy's illness and hoped a visit to the church would lift her spiritually. However, she was so drunk that she barely understood her own actions. She pounded her fists angrily on the front door to the cathedral, but it was locked. Veronica cried in vain for the "Mother of God" to help her, screaming hysterically until a policeman escorted her away. By that time, she had reached the rectory door and cried on the steps, mumbling for a priest to come out and save her. The policeman took Veronica away to the local station, where she was fined twenty-five dollars and jailed for the evening.

She lived in fear of Andy's death; when he died she would be destitute and alone for the first time in her life. She had vague thoughts of running away, of moving to another country or state. As with other schizophrenics, she fit the pattern perfectly: fleeing from her problems was the easy way out. And like other alcoholics, what she wanted was at least unawareness, if not oblivion.

In the fall of 1965, she relocated to Florida. Veronica said she wanted "the sun and easy life," and established residency in the city of Tampa Bay. Andy always seemed to find her. He was still working despite his illness, and one afternoon when his boat landed in Tampa Bay, he paid a call on Veronica. It was the first time she had seen him in almost four months. He appeared more haggard than ever, so weak that he had barely enough strength to tie his shoes. Veronica did her best to care for Andy, keeping him with her through Christmas. Before Andy shipped off again, a short time afterward, they made plans to meet in New York in March.

But he didn't make it. Andy called Veronica in February and told her he had returned from his trip early. He was feeling weaker and he was now living in a small, run-down apartment on the outskirts of the Bronx. Veronica flew to New York to join him, planning to move in to help care for him. She had had second thoughts about leaving him to suffer alone. She heard the dragging of his feet when he came to answer the door, and she saw that his legs were bloated and stiff as he walked. She was shocked to see how much he had failed.

Veronica had him examined at the Merchant Marine Hospital on Staten Island. The doctor reported that Andy was suffering from a combination of health problems—his liver, his spleen, his kidney, and bladder were all malfunctioning. The doctor said he could save Andy if he agreed to surgery—*and* stayed off the booze. Andy violently rejected such an idea, and his health further deteriorated.

By early September, his arms and legs were so weak that he couldn't even carry a bag of groceries or climb the stairs to the apartment. When his condition turned critical, Veronica informed Andy's mother and sister in Wisconsin to come fast; they flew in to be with him during his final hours.

On September 18, 1965, Andy was in such excruciating pain that he was admitted to the hospital. Veronica saw him before the ambulance arrived. She kissed him on the forehead and squeezed his hand affectionately before he was taken away, telling him not to worry and predicting a full recovery. But the next day, Andy was pronounced dead, and Veronica was the last to know. The doctor phoned the following afternoon with his condolences, but by then, funeral arrangements had already been completed. Andy's body was shipped to Wisconsin and was buried before Veronica could even send one white rose to be placed on his casket.

With word that Andy's body had been interred, Veronica suffered an emotional breakdown. She was devastated over the news. He was all she had. Veronica saw no reason to live. She vowed to join Andy wherever he was.

19

· · · ·

The Final Days

NOTHING MATTERED. She drank around the clock. Her children were all on their own, so she didn't have them to lean on for support. André was living in Switzerland and his alimony payments were his only contact with her.

Lake stuck around New York for several more months after Andy's death, through Christmas and early January. She was still attached to the Manhattan skyline and the good times she had shared with Andy. Most of her hours were spent bar-hopping. None of the patrons ever associated her with the glamorous movie-star, Veronica Lake. Her once-famous hair was often unwashed and had tinges of gray and her face was more bloated than before. She was overweight and her teeth were stained.

There was nobody to help her, but then again, she didn't want any help. She had always felt that nobody understood her and that she was better off alone. Her drinking resulted in sleeping off hangovers on barroom floors or walking the streets for handouts. She had sunk as low as possible.

According to Helene, Veronica was in terrible shape. Her three previous marriages were still scars from the past. Her mother was still not talking to her; alcohol was her only companion. Money was also in short supply. Helene relates: "Her self-esteem was so low that it was hard to bring her back to reality. She was still in that little world of hers, more so than before. Finally, she went back to her mother for fifty cents here, a dollar, or more. But Constance didn't know how to help her. It would have taken a lot of patience and it wasn't going to be easy helping that type of mind. Veronica knew she needed help, but was just unsure what to do. So she went to her mother."

Veronica was like a battered baby bird returning to the nest. She didn't beg forgiveness, but Constance welcomed her anyway. Mrs. Keane had always cared for her daughter, through thick and thin, even though Veronica never quite saw it that way. She always believed that Constance was hanging on to the coattails of her success, enriching her own pocketbook off "Veronica Lake, the movie star." Mrs. Keane's version is that Veronica never understood her intentions from the beginning, because she was always "a very disturbed girl."

Constance also remembers that her renewed relationship with Veronica wasn't always easy. "Veronica always associated with low-grade people. Whenever she was over, she was always drinking. One of her friends, who was also over one time, said to her, 'Why don't you stop all of this nonsense with the drinking?' She said, 'Never, I like it this way.' She stayed overnight and the next day she was sitting on the floor with a turkey out of the refrigerator and a can of beer. I said, 'My, God, don't drink that.' She said, 'Oh, it's good for your stomach.' You just couldn't talk to her."

Constance tried mending the long feud with Veronica by inviting her over for Christmas dinner, but Veronica read her the riot act for the umpteenth time. "I could always tell by her voice that she was under the weather. 'What did you ever do for me?' I'd say, 'Connie, I have a present under the tree. Wouldn't you like to come over?' She'd say scornfully, 'I'm not coming to your goddamn house now or any other time.' The next day, she would show up as if nothing happened."

Whenever she wasn't with her mother, Veronica drifted in and out of the bars, sometimes sleeping in them, since she was often evicted from hotels for lack of rent. Once, when she had not paid her rent, the hotel locked her out of her room. The next day, she was discovered fast asleep in the boiler room. Another time, Mrs. Keane received a phone call late at night from a bar downtown. Veronica was in the Colonnade Room lying on the floor, completely passed out, while everybody was stepping over her.

Veronica kept visiting her mother periodically, mostly for money or handouts, until she finally packed her belongings and moved back to Florida. Constance believes that her daughter was resigned to being ill, drunk, unhappy, and doomed. "I used to dread reading the newspaper because I didn't know what was going to turn up next on her."

Veronica rented an apartment near the outskirts of Hollywood, Florida. She had very little money, as her only source of income was her alimony payments from her ex-husbands. In the spring of 1966 she received a call from a Canadian film company interested in starring her in an ultra-low budget horror film, *Footsteps in the Snow.* The story dealt with "dope traffic and ski bums" and, needing the money, Veronica agreed to the offer. She made enough to hold her over for several more months, with most of it supporting her alcoholism. The film was released later that same year, but it was a bomb.

Then, in early June, Lake received another phone call. This time, it was from the Gallery Restaurant Playhouse in Miami. The owner wanted Veronica to headline in the playhouse production of *Goodbye Charlie.* Her pay would be $1,250 a week. Veronica had no agent and wasn't interested in working much anymore. But she took the job.

The Florida news media hyped her first stage appearance to the hilt. Press corp members were on hand to greet her at her first rehearsal, asking questions on her return to acting. One reporter wrote, "Her hair was knotted on top of her head in a dark blonde tangle. Flesh-colored band-aids were taped to several fingers. The only makeup on her face was a touch of lipstick and her complexion looked pasty in the bright sunlight."

Goodbye Charlie opened, after weeks of rehearsals, on June 4, 1966, to mixed reviews. The *Miami-Herald* said: "The talent and personal magnetism of one-time movie great Veronica Lake have not run dry." Veronica said she had found this first taste of acting in some time enjoyable, but that she was very uncomfortable as well. She stored several bottles of vodka in her dressing room and between rehearsals or performances, she would sneak back for a hefty gulp. The show lasted only two weeks.

When Veronica wasn't working, she became a prize celebrity in the city's homosexual bars. She was a great supporter of the gay movement and spent most of her time with her homosexual acquaintances.

Veronica had earned enough to hold her over for most of the year, but it didn't brighten her attitude toward life. But at least it meant that she didn't have to worry about how she was going to be able to buy the next drink. She stacked up four or five cases of vodka each week outside the side entrance to her apartment. Helene Nielsen explains that Veronica, like most alcoholics, was unaware about what alcohol was doing to her. "Veronica couldn't fight back. Her excuse was to die drinking. She might have listened to people if she had been taken out of this situation and placed in a different environment. But Veronica couldn't take that. She ran. She got to the point where she wouldn't listen. Her attitude got so bad that she didn't even get dressed. She didn't even bathe. She was definitely over the deep end. It would have taken a long time to have helped her."

By the winter of 1968, she was so spent every day that she could barely talk on the phone or perform any of her daily functions. Richard Webb remembers visiting the actress while shooting a television show in the Florida area. Webb reneged on an offer to join her for a drink: "On the side entrance to her apartment, there were four cases of vodka stacked on top of one another. Veronica guzzled it down in no time. She started drinking at ten o'clock in the morning, and greeted her guests with a typical hug and remark, 'Have a drink.' I said, 'No, Connie, I don't do that anymore.' Her hair was pulled back and she had begun to sag a little by then."

Not only had she stopped her sporadic attempts at personal grooming, but Veronica became so lethargic that she also neglected the responsibilities of her work. Several months later, she was approached by producer Brad Grinter to star in his low-budget horror film, *Flesh Feast.* Veronica accepted the offer to star and direct the vehicle as well. It was her second quickie production in four years and was also shot in Miami. Lake played the austere Dr. Elaine Frederick, who had recently been released from a Florida mental institution. The plot centered around a youth restoration process, using preconditioned flesh-eating maggots.

Grinter, who was the cousin of actor Richard Webb, recalls that Veronica had to sleep off the effects of her drinking from the night before. Her hangovers usually resulted in her being late to the set. Richard Webb remembers asking Grinter, " 'How does Veronica look?' He said, 'She's got a face like an angel.' I then said, 'Is she easy to work with?' He said, 'Yeah, if you start shooting in the afternoon.' " *Flesh Feasts* was her final appearance on the screen. It was released three years later and made satisfactory returns in the action-market cinemas. The film lasted three days in Los Angeles.

Veronica's days in Florida were also numbered. She was convinced that people were spying on her. She even thought the FBI was tapping her phone. Lake was so paranoid that she couldn't survive closed up in her little apartment; it only compounded her anxieties and furthered her frustrations.

In the summer of 1969, Veronica found the solution when she relocated to the port city of Ipswich, England. She rented a small apartment and found her change in venue was just what the doctor had ordered. The people of this small city were friendly and had a kind word whenever she needed one. At the time, she said, "I find England so relaxing after the turmoil of living in America. And I plan to make my life here. Here people seem to be more on my own wavelength and take my remarks in the spirit they're intended." Lake's cousin backs up that claim. "I think it was the coolness of the people and the fact they didn't intrude on her privacy. They also didn't expect too much from her. She respected them, and they respected her. They wanted to help her, and that's why she liked England so much."

One of her first priorities was to enlist the services of

a collaborator named Donald Bain, who helped ghost write her autobiography, *Veronica*. Published in England in the spring of 1969, the book drew such rave reviews in the United Kingdom that it created renewed interest in her personally and professionally. The book was given critical acclaim for its candidness, even though Veronica, as always, let her imagination run wild at times.

Consequently, offers came pouring in. Her first one came in late June from the stage company producing a new English version of *Madame Chairman*. Lake's salary was $1,250 a week. She portrayed Lady Louise Peverall, a seemingly scatterbrained American widow, who takes over her English husband's business interests and proves that she was really the dynamo behind the man. Her first appearance on the London stage caused quite a stir among members of the press. Newspaper reporters rushed to the theater to interview this fading glamour queen. In these articles, Veronica was described as "frank, a hard-working individual, who drank a bit much, but was up for the rigorous part."

During tryouts, Veronica suffered a back injury, as she was completely out of shape. Afterward, she announced, "My back may be killing me, but at least I won't die of boredom."

Following *Madame Chairman*'s opening in July 1969, newspapers reported that the show was having technical problems that were affecting the show's slick performance. In an interview, Veronica discussed these setbacks and her attempts to deal with them:

> If this goddamned play is going to make it in the West End, I want it to come in with dignity. I've got to pull this company together. I've put so much of my own money into this show, I feel like an angel. I'm rewrit-

ing the script every day and paying a stenographer out of my own pocket to type the changes so these kids [her co-players] will have time to learn their new lines. You don't know how many times I've wanted to walk out on this show. But I couldn't jeopardize the jobs of ten other actors. But this goddamned company is the most mismanaged I've ever seen.

But in spite of all of Veronica's efforts, the show folded.

In the fall of 1969, Veronica renewed her bid to star on stage in the play *A Streetcar Named Desire*. Directed by David Poulson, the play opened at the New Theatre in Bromley, Kent, for three weeks, starting on September 8, 1969. Co-starring opposite Lake was ex-television western hero, Ty Hardin. The pay was paltry, only two hundred fifty dollars a week, but the critics were mostly kind to Veronica. Roberta Ghisays, in her review for Reuters, wrote that "Miss Lake appeared nervous at first in the taxing role of the unfortunate Blanche DuBois, but she gained confidence as the evening progressed and showed the heroine's final mental breakdown movingly."

Lake told Ghisays after the show that the DuBois character was quite a challenge, one that she couldn't have possibly essayed ten years earlier. As she confessed: "I hope I've developed and progressed a bit since then. I've learned a great deal from many gifted people. And if I have nothing else to show for my life, apart from a scrapbook full of faded clippings, I have the knowledge that my early days in Hollywood weren't in vain."

Lake continued to live in Ipswich until March 1971, at which time her book, *Veronica*, was published in the United States by Citadel Press. The republication prompted a whirlwind tour through New York and Hollywood. It was her return to Hollywood that captured most of the attention. Her appearances on the various television and radio talk shows were candid, to say the least. She came across as a tough broad who enjoyed her life as a nostalgic martyr. Her face reflected her less than pristine past; she told one reporter, "I earned this face." Her figure was heavier, and her husky voice still used plenty of expletives. When questioned on whether alcohol had greatly affected her life, she remarked, "To each his own. I'm not a mainliner and it's more fun getting high without a needle. At least, you can get over booze."

At this point in her life, Lake also preferred referring to herself as "a former sex zombie" rather than sex symbol. "That really names me properly. I was laughing at everybody in all of my portraits. I never took that stuff seriously."

In April 1971, Veronica made her well-publicized return to Hollywood to ballyhoo her book. She was astonished over the changes in the city during her absence. She paid a visit to the old Paramount lot on Bronson Avenue, her first in over twenty years, only to find that most of her memories had been stripped away. She had hoped the visit would do her some good, but instead she left crying. A fountain that had stood in the backlot had been torn out and the casting office had been relocated and painted over. Turning every corner, her legs weakened on her as she sobbed endlessly. Where had all the memories gone? As she told one reporter: "I hardly recognize it, the way they've changed everything."

Later that same day, she was collared by Virginia Graham, then queen of the television talk-show circuit, whom she told, "If I had stayed in Hollywood, I would have ended up like Alan Ladd and Gail Russell, dead and buried by now. That rat race killed them and I knew it would eventually kill me. So I had to get out. I wasn't psychologically meant to be a picture star. I never took it seriously. I hated being something I wasn't. You know, everybody thinks I ran out on Hollywood because my career was going downhill. I left to save my life."

Veronica kept drinking in the seclusion of her Hollywood hotel room, sobering up right before the telecasts. Teet Carle remembers when she was a guest on *The Merv Griffin Show,* she clearly showed that she was under the influence. "She looked ill-at-ease when she came out, and sounded embarrassed to talk about what had happened to her. She acted sort of tentative about things, and the way I remember it, she said, 'When I came back, I wanted to return to the Paramount lot to walk around and have all the good memories come back to me—the fountain with the goldfish, my dressing room—but when I went out there, Thomas Wolfe was right, 'You can't go home again.' "

Los Angeles radio personality Gary Owens interviewed Lake on his show for radio station KMPC. Beforehand, Owens was asked to meet Veronica, along with Sue Cameron of the *Hollywood Reporter,* for lunch at the Hamburger Hamlet, across from Grauman's Chinese Theatre where Lake's star is located in the Hollywood Walk of Fame. His impressions of that meeting and of her were as follows:

I had always been a fan of hers, and found her very charming and not evasive at all. She wore a minimum amount of makeup, and her complexion was ruddy from boozing it all the time. She was very candid, though. If I asked her what so-and-so was like to work with, for instance, she'd say, "Oh, he was such an ass." It wasn't so surprising to hear such salty language come out of her mouth as it would have been during the golden years when she was dolled up in makeup and long satin dresses. Of course, her bloated face added a certain toughness that made her volatile language acceptable.

Owens recalled that Veronica appeared bitter about her years in Hollywood, anxious at being back at the scene where she suffered many years of turmoil. Lake still spoke unfavorably about the relationship with her mother, as Owens relates: "Veronica was still talking about the time her mother sued her. It seemed to really bother her because her mother claimed she had abandoned her. But Veronica felt she hadn't. The scars of the incident were still evident."

Between radio and television interviews, Veronica stayed at the Ambassador Hotel in Hollywood. She encouraged former associates and friends to come over and join her for drinks. Richard Webb, who called to congratulate Lake on the Griffin show, recalls that her taste for booze was still a high priority. "Veronica's greeting on the phone was, 'Hey, you ol' son of a bitch, how are you?' I said, 'Fine.' Then, she insisted, 'Come on down, let's have a drink.' I reminded her that I didn't drink and that she should stop before it was too late. She said, 'Not me, I'm going to die drinking.' "

She did. Veronica returned to Ipswich, England, and, in June 1972, she was married a fourth time, to Robert Carlton-Monroe, a sea captain with the Royal Navy. That marriage ended in divorce the following year.

Then, on July 7, 1973, the same week death claimed the lives of Lon Chaney, Jr. and Betty Grable, Veronica succumbed to acute hepatitis. Visiting in the United States, Lake had been admitted to a hospital in Vermont when she complained about severe pains in her kidneys. She was fifty-one.

She died penniless, alone, and without friends. But at

least the hell of living was over for her. As Constance recalls today: "I'm glad she died when she did, it would have only gotten worse. In my opinion, she committed professional suicide. She killed herself with her drinking."

Veronica's funeral was held in a Manhattan chapel. She was cremated and her remains were spread over the Atlantic Ocean. All of her so-called friends failed to show, as well as any of her four husbands, two daughters, and her mother. None of them came. (Mrs. Keane had been advised by friends that it would not be in her best interests to attend.)

Only Michael flew in from Hawaii with his wife. But Michael couldn't persuade André De Toth, his wealthy father, to lend him the money for the funeral. According to Michael, André declined and called his son obscene names for even bothering him. DeToth retorted he never went to his mother's funeral, so why should he go to Veronica's?

Understandably, Michael was bitter over the whole situation. His wife and he took out a five-hundred-dollar bank loan to help cover expenses for the funeral and their trip. As he told one reporter at the scene: "Everyone wanted to offer me a hand except my own family. When I saw my mother's body at the hospital morgue, I was heartbroken. She looked so small and lonely."

Even though he saw her infrequently, Michael explains that "I never stopped loving her, and I'm sure she never stopped loving me. She understood that her world was not my world, but I did write to her regularly. Unfortunately, I didn't know she was ill until it was too late."

Shortly before her death, Veronica had called her editor at Citadel Press, Allan J. Wilson, asking him to assess any royalties due her from her autobiography.

Wilson told her, "None, Veronica. You have none coming."

Sounding weary, she pleaded, "Allan, could you loan me two hundred dollars. I promise to pay you back."

Considering her past reputation with bills, Wilson said he would, but dispatched a letter along with the payment for her to sign stating that she would reimburse the money in thirty days.

Two weeks later, Wilson received news that Veronica was dead. The following week, he received a call from Lake's fourth husband, Robert. Carlton was compiling Lake's assets and wanted to know if her book had grossed any further royalties.

Wilson said, "No, it hasn't but can you do me a favor?"

Carlton asked, "What's that?"

"Could you pay me the two hundred dollars Veronica still owes me?"

Filmography*

(All films are black and white unless otherwise noted. Role follows cast listing.)

AS CONSTANCE KEANE:

THE WRONG ROOM (RKO, released September 22, 1939). Running Time: 19 minutes/*Producer:* Bert Gilroy/ *Director:* Lou Brock/ *Story:* Stanley Rauh and Lou Brock/ *Cast:* Leon Errol, Ed Dunn, Charlotte Treadway, and John Laing/ "Daughter of Professor Errol."

SORORITY HOUSE (RKO, released May 5, 1939). Running Time: 64 minutes/ *Producer:* Robert Sisk/ *Director:* John Farrow/ *Story:* Mary Coyle Chase/ *Cast:* Anne Shirley, James Ellison, Barbara Read, Pamela Blake, J.M. Kerrigan,

Compiled by Greg Lenburg.

Helen Wood, Doris Jordan, June Storey, Elisabeth Risdon, Margaret Armstrong, Selmer Jackson, and Chill Wills/ "Sorority Girl."

ALL WOMEN HAVE SECRETS (Paramount, released December 15, 1939). Running Time: 74 minutes/ *Producer:* Edward T. Lowe/ *Director:* Kurt Neumann/ *Story:* Dale Eunson/ *Cast:* Jeanne Cagney, Joseph Allen, Jr., Virginia Dale, Peter Hayes, Betty Moran, John Arledge, Lawrence Grossmith, Una O'Connor, Billy Lee, George Meeker, Wanda McKay, and Fay McKenzie/ "College Girl"/ *Working title:* Campus Wives.

YOUNG AS YOU FEEL (Twentieth Century Fox, released February 16, 1940). Running Time: 59 minutes/ *Associate Producer:* John Stone/ *Director:* Malcolm St. Clair/ *Screenplay:* Joseph Hoffman and Stanley Rauh/ *Cast:* Jed Pouty, Spring Byington, Joan Valerie, Russell Gleason, Kenneth Howell, George Ernest, June Carlson, Florence Roberts, William Mahan, Helen Ericson, George Givot, Marvin Stephens, Harlan Briggs, Harry Shannon, Jack Carson, Guy Repp, Brodelet Esther, Gladys Blake, Irma Wilson, John Sheehan, Lee Shumway, John H. Elliott, Bruce Warren, and Joan Leslie/ "Girl"/ Also known as *The Jones Family in Young As You Feel.*

FORTY LITTLE MOTHERS (MGM, released April 26, 1940). Running Time: 90 minutes/ *Producer:* Harry Rapf/ *Director:* Busby Berkeley/ *Screenplay:* Dorothy Yost and Ernest Pagono/ *Cast:* Eddie Cantor, Judith Anderson, Rita Johnson, Bonita Granville, Diana Lewis, Nydia Westman, Ralph Morgan, Martha O'Driscoll, Charlotte Munier, Eva Puig, Louise Seidel, Margaret Early, Barbara Quintanilla, and Richard Cramer/ "Classmate."

AS VERONICA LAKE:

I WANTED WINGS (Paramount, released May 30, 1941). Running Time: 135 minutes/ *Producer:* Arthur Hornblow, Jr./ *Director:* Mitchell Leisen/ *Screenplay:* Richard Maibum, Lieutenant B. Lay, Jr., and Sid Herzig/ *Cast:* Ray Milland, William Holden, Wayne Morris, Brian Donlevy, Constance Moore, Harry Davenport, Phil Brown, Edward Fielding, Willard Robertson, Richard Lane, Addison Richards, Hobart Cavanaugh, Douglas Aylesworth, John Trent, Archie Twitchell, Richard Webb, John Hiestand, Lane Chandler, and Alan Hale, Jr./ "Sally Vaughn"/ Academy Award, Best Special Effects.

HOLD BACK THE DAWN (Paramount, released September 26, 1941). Running Time: 116 minutes/ *Producer:* Arthur Hornblow, Jr./ *Director:* Mitchell Leisen/ *Screenplay:* Charles Brackett and Billy Wilder/ *Cast:* Charles Boyer, Olivia De Havilland, Paulette Goddard, Victor Francen, Walter Abel, Curt Bois, Rosemary DeCamp, Eric Feldary, Nestor Paiva, Eva Puig, Micheline Cheirel, Madeleine LeBeau, Billy Lee, Mikhail Rasumny, Mitchell Leisen, Brian Donlevy, Richard Webb, Sonny Boy Williams, Edward Fielding, Don Douglas, Gertrude Astor, Carlos Villarias, Arthur Loft, Charles Arnt, Ella Neal, Ray Mala, June Wilkins, Leon Belasco, and Chester Clute/ "Actress."

SULLIVAN'S TRAVELS (Paramount, released February 6, 1942; © December 4, 1941). Running Time: 90 minutes/ *Producer:* Paul Jones/ *Director-Story-Screenplay:* Preston Sturges/ *Cast:* Joel McCrea, Robert Warwick, William Demarest, Franklin Pangborn, Porter Hall, Byron Foulger, Margaret Hayes, Robert Greig, Eric Blore, Torben Meyer, Victor Potel, Richard Webb, Charles Moore, Almira Sessions, Esther Howard, Frank Moran, George Renavent,

Harry Rosenthal, Alan Bridge, Jimmy Conlin, Jan Buckingham, Robert Winkler, Chick Collins, Jimmie Dundee, Roscoe Ates, Monte Blue, Emory Parnell, Billy Bletcher, and Chester Conklin/ "The Girl."

THIS GUN FOR HIRE (Paramount, released June 19, 1942). Running Time: 81 minutes/ *Producer:* Richard M. Blumenthal/ *Director:* Frank Tuttle/ *Screenplay:* Albert Waltz and W.R. Burnett/ *Cast:* Robert Preston, Laird Cregar, Alan Ladd, Tully Marshall, Marc Lawrence, Olin Howlin, Roger Imhof, Pamela Blake, Frank Ferguson, Victor Kilian, Patricia Farr, Harry Shannon, Charles C. Wilson, Mikhail Rasumny, Bernadene Hayes, Mary Davenport, Chester Clute, Charles Arnt, Earle Dewey, Clem Bevans, Lynda Grey, Virita Campbell, Tim Ryan, Pat O'Malley, Richard Webb, and Yvonne DeCarlo/ "Ellen Graham."

THE GLASS KEY (Paramount, release date not available; © October 26, 1942). Running Time: 85 minutes/ *Producer:* Fred Kohlmar/ *Director:* Stuart Heisler/ *Screenplay:* Jonathan Latimer/ *Cast:* Brian Donlevy, Alan Ladd, Bonita Granville, Richard Denning, Joseph Calleia, William Bendix, Frances Gifford, Donald MacBride, Margaret Hayes, Moroni Olsen, Eddie Marr, Arthur Loft, George Meader, Pat O'Malley, Vernon Dent, Lillian Randolph, and William Benedict/ "Janet Henry"/ Remake of the original 1935 film.

I MARRIED A WITCH (UA, released October 30, 1942). Running Time: 76 minutes/ *Producer-Director:* Rene Clair/ *Screenplay:* Robert Pirosh and Marc Connelly/ *Cast:* Frederic March, Robert Benchley, Susan Hayward, Cecil Kellaway, Elizabeth Patterson, Robert Warwick, Eily Maylon, Robert Greig, Viola Moore, Mary Field, Nora Cecil, Emory

Parnell, Helen St. Rayner, Aldrich Bowker, Emma Dunn, Billy Bletcher, Chester Conklin, Monte Blue, Billy Bevan, and Reed Hadley/ "Jennifer"/ Filmed at Paramount.

STAR SPANGLED RHYTHM (Paramount, released February 12, 1943 © December 29, 1942). Running Time: 99 minutes/ *Associate Producer:* Joseph Sistrom/ *Director:* George Marshall/ *Screenplay:* Harry Tugend/ *Cast:* Bing Crosby, Bob Hope, Fred MacMurray, Franchot Tone, Ray Milland, Victor Moore, Dorothy Lamour, Paulette Goddard, Vera Zorina, Marion Martin, Dick Powell, Betty Hutton, Eddie Bracken, Eddie Anderson, William Bendix, Jerry Colonna, Susan Hayward, Arthur Treacher, Sterling Holloway, and Julie Gibson/ 'Peekaboo Bang' in "Sweater (Paulette Goddard), Sarong (Dorothy Lamour), and a Peekaboo Bang" number.

SO PROUDLY WE HAIL (Paramount, released June 6, 1943). Running Time: 125 minutes/ *Producer-Director:* Mark Sandrich/ *Screenplay:* Allan Scott/ *Cast:* Claudette Colbert, Paulette Goddard, George Reeves, Barbara Britton, Walter Abel, Sonny Tufts, Mary Servoss, Ted Hecht, John Litel, Dr. Hugh Ho Chung, Mary Treen, Kitty Kelly, Helen Lynd, Lorna Gray, Dorothy Adams, Ann Doran, Jean Willes, Lynn Walker, Joan Tours, Jan Wiley, Mimi Doyle, James Bell, Dick Hogan, Bill Goodwin, James Flavin, Byron Foulger, Elsa Janssen, Richard Crane, Boyd Davis, Will Wright, William Forrest, Frances Morris, and Yvonne DeCarlo/ "Lieutenant Olivia D'Arcy"/ Working Title: *Hands of Mercy.*

THE HOUR BEFORE THE DAWN (Paramount, release date not available; © March 24, 1944). Running Time: 74 minutes/ *Associate Producer:* William Dozier/ *Director:* Frank Tuttle/

Screenplay: Michael Hogan/ *Cast:* Franchot Tone, John Sutton, Binnie Barnes, Henry Stephenson, Phillip Merivale, Nils Asther, Edmond Breon, David Leland, Aminta Dyne, Morton Lowry, Ivan Simpson, Donald Stuart, Henry Allen, Mary Gordon, Ernest Severn, Raymond Severn, Leslie Denison, Harry Cording, Hilda Plowright, Viola Moore, David Clyde, Tempe Pigott, Marjean Neville, Marie deBecker, Thomas Louden, Deidre Gale, Nigel Morton, Otto Reichow, and Charles H. Faber/ "Dora Bruckmann."

BRING ON THE GIRLS (Paramount, released February 17, 1945). Running Time: 92 minutes/ *Associate Producer:* Fred Kohlmar/ *Director:* Sidney Lanfield/ *Screenplay:* Karl Tunberg and Darrell Ware/ *Cast:* Sonny Tufts, Eddie Bracken, Marjorie Reynolds, Grant Mitchell, Johnnie Coy, Peter Whitney, Alan Mowbray, Porter Hall, Thurston Hall, Lloyd Corrigan, Sig Arno, Joan Woodbury, Andrew Tombes, Frank Faylen, Huntz Hall, William Moss, Norma Varden, The Golden Gate Quartette, Spike Jones and His Orchestra, Marietta Canty, Dorothea Kent, Ray Riggs, Stan Johnson, William Haade, Jimmie Dundee, Walter Baldwin, Pat Cameron, Maxine Fife, Veda Ann Borg, Douglas Walton, Grant Withers, Noel Neill, Jimmy Conlin, Yvonne DeCarlo, and Jimmy Dodd/ "Teddy Collins."

OUT OF THIS WORLD (Paramount, released July 13, 1945). Running Time: 96 minutes/ *Associate Producer:* Sam Coslow/ *Director:* Hal Walker/ *Screenplay:* Walter DeLeon and Arthur Phillips/ *Cast:* Eddie Bracken, Diana Lynn, Cass Daley, Parkyakarkus, Donald MacBride, Florence Bates, Gary Crosby, Phillip Crosby, Dennis Crosby, Lin Crosby, Olga San Juan, Nancy Porter, Audrey Young, Carol Deere, Carmen Cavallaro, Ted Fiorito, Henry King, Ray Noble, Joe Reichman, Don Wilson, Mabel Paige, Charles Smith, and Irving Bacon/ "Dorothy Dudge"/ Bracken's singing voice is that of Bing Crosby's.

DUFFY'S TAVERN (Paramount, released September 28, 1945). Running Time: 98 minutes/ *Associate Producer:* Danny Dare/ *Director:* Hal Walker/ *Screenplay:* Melvin Frank and Norman Panama/ *Cast:* Bing Crosby, Betty Hutton, Paulette Goddard, Alan Ladd, Dorothy Lamour, Eddie Bracken, Sonny Tufts, Arturo DeCordova, Cass Daley, Diana Lynn, Gary Crosby, Phillip Crosby, Dennis Crosby, Lidsay Crosby, William Bendix, Joan Caulfield, Gail Russell, Barry Fitzgerald, Marjorie Reynolds, Barry Sullivan, Howard Da Silva, Billy De Wolfe, Walter Abel, Olga San Juan, Frank Faylen, Matt McHugh, Noel Neill, and many others/ Cameo in a mystery segment with Alan Ladd; deleted was a scene with the Crosby Boys and actress Julie Gibson.

HOLD THAT BLONDE (Paramount, released November 23, 1945). Running Time: 76 minutes/ *Producer:* Paul Jones/ *Director:* George Marshall/ *Screenplay:* Walter DeLeon, Earl Baldwin, and E. Edwin Moran/ *Cast:* Eddie Bracken, Albert Dekker, Frank Fenton, George Zucco, Donald MacBride, Lewis L. Russell, Norma Varden, Ralph Peters, Robert Watson, Lyle Latell, Edmund MacDonald, Willie Best, Jack Norton, and Eddie Laughton/ "Sally Martin"/ Working title: *Good Intentions.*

MISS SUSIE SLAGLE'S (Paramount, released March 8, 1946). Running Time: 88 minutes *Associate Producer:* John Houseman/ *Director:* John Berry/ *Screenplay:* Walter DeLeon/ *Cast:* Sonny Tufts, Joan Caulfield, Ray Collins, Billy De Wolfe, Bill Edwards, Pat Phelan, Lillian Gish, Roman Bohnen, Morris Carnovsky, Renny McEvoy, Lloyd Bridges, Michael

Sage, Dorothy Adams, E.J. Ballatine, Theodore Newton, J. Lewis Johnson, Ludwig Stossel, Charles E. Arnt, Isabel Randolph, and Kathleen Howard/ "Nan Rogers."

THE BLUE DAHLIA (Paramount, released April 19, 1946). 99 minutes/ *Producer:* George Marshall/ *Associate Producer:* John Houseman/ *Director:* George Marshall/ *Screenplay:* Raymond Chandler/ *Cast:* Alan Ladd, William Bendix, Howard Da Silva, Doris Dowling, Tom Powers, Hugh Beaumont, Howard Freeman, Don Costello, Will Wright, Frank Faylen, Walter Sande, Mae Busch, George Barton, Matt McHugh, Noel Neill, and Milton Kibbee/ "Joyce Harwood."

RAMROD (UA, released May 2, 1946). Running Time: 94 minutes/ *Producer:* Harry Sherman/ *Director:* André De Toth/ *Screenplay:* Jack Moffitt/ *Cast:* Joel McCrea, Ian MacDonald, Charlie Ruggles, Preston Foster, Arleen Whelan, Lloyd Bridges, Donald Crisp, Rose Higgins, Chick York, Sarah Padden, Trevor Bardette, Don DeFore, Nestor Paiva, Cliff Parkinson, John Powers, Ward Wood, Hal Taliaferro, Wally Cassell, Ray Teal, and Jeff Corey/ "Connie Dickason."

VARIETY GIRL (Paramount, released August 29, 1946). Running Time: 93 minutes/ *Producer:* Daniel Dare/ *Director:* George Marshall/ *Screenplay:* Edmund Hartman, Frank Tashlin, Robert Welch, and Monte Brice/ *Cast:* Mary Hatcher, Olga San Juan, De Forest Kelley, Bing Crosby, Bob Hope, Gary Cooper, Ray Milland, Alan Ladd, Barbara Stanwyck, Paulette Goddard, Dorothy Lamour, Sonny Tufts, Joan Caulfield, William Holden, Lizabeth Scott, Burt Lancaster, Gail Russell, Diana Lynn, Sterling Hayden, Robert Preston, John Lund, William Bendix, Barry Fitzgerald, Cass Daley, Howard Da Silva, Billy De Wolfe, McDonald

Carey, Arleen Whelan, Patric Knowles, William Demarest, Mona Freeman, Cecil Kellaway, Johnnie Coy, Virginia Field, Richard Webb, Stanley Clements, Frank Faylen, Frank Ferguson, Cecil B. DeMille, Mitchell Leisen, Frank Butler, George Marshall, Roger Dann, Pearl Bailey, The Mulcays, Spike Jones and His City Slickers, and many others/ "Herself"/ Featured is a special color sequence with George Pal's Puppetoons.

SAIGON (Paramount, released March 12, 1948). Running Time: 94 minutes/ *Producer:* P.J. Wolfson/ *Director:* Leslie Fenton/ *Screenplay:* P.J. Wolfson and Arthur Sheekman/ *Cast:* Alan Ladd, Douglas Dick, Wally Cassell, Luther Adler, Morris Carnovsky, Mikhail Rasumny, Luis Van Rooten, Eugene Borden, and Griff Barnett/ "Susan Cleaver."

THE SAINTED SISTERS (Paramount, released April 30, 1948). Running Time: 90 minutes/ *Producer:* Richard Maibum/ *Director:* William D. Russell/ *Screenplay:* Harry Clork and N. Richard Nash/ *Cast:* Joan Caulfield, Barry Fitzgerald, William Demarest, George Reeves, Beulah Bondi, Chill Wills, Darryl Hickman, Jimmy Hunt, Kathryn Card, Ray Walker, Harold Vermilyea, Hank Worden, and Milt Kibbee/ "Letty Stanton."

ISN'T IT ROMANTIC? (Paramount, released October 8, 1948). Running Time: 88 minutes/ *Producer:* Daniel Dare/ *Director:* Norman Z. McLeod/ *Screenplay:* Theodore Strauss, Joseph Mischel, and Richard L. Breen/ *Cast:* Mona Freeman, Mary Hatcher, Billy De Wolfe, Roland Culver, Patric Knowles, Richard Webb, Kathryn Givney, Larry Olsen, and Pearl Bailey/ "Candy"/ Working titles: *Father's Day* and *It's Always Spring.*

SLATTERY'S HURRICANE (Twentieth Century Fox, released August 6, 1949). Running Time: 83 minutes/ *Producer:* William Perlberg/ *Director:* André De Toth/ *Screenplay:* Herman Wouk and Richard Murphy/ *Cast:* Richard Widmark, Linda Darnell, John Russell, Gary Merrill, Walter Kingsford, Raymond Greenleaf, Stanley Waxman, Joseph De Santis, and Dick Wessel/ "Dolores."

STRONGHOLD (Lippert, released February 15, 1952). Running Time: 78 minutes/ *Producer:* Robert Lippert/ *Director:* Steve Sekeley/ *Screenplay:* Wells Root/ *Cast:* Zachary Scott, Arturo de Cordova, Rita Macedo, Fanny Schiller, Gilberto Gonzalez, Gustavo Rojo, and Irene Ajay/ "Mary Stevens"/ Filmed in Mexico.

FOOTSTEPS IN THE SNOW (Evergreen Film Productions, released October 27, 1966). Running time not available/ color/ *Director:* Martin Green/ *Cast:* Ovila Legare and Meredith MacRae/ role unavailable/ Filmed in Quebec, Canada; received limited American distribution with English subtitles.

FLESH FEAST (Viking International, released January 4, 1973). Running Time: 72 minutes/ color/ *Producers:* Veronica Lake and Brad F. Grinter/ *Director:* Brad F. Grinter/ *Screenplay:* Thomas Casey/ *Cast:* Phil Philbin, Martha Mischon, Dian Wilhite, Heather Hughes, Yanka Mann, and Chris Mitchell/ "Dr. Elaine Frederick"/ Also known as *Time for Terror;* filmed in Florida.

Radio

(The following is a list of Veronica Lake's appearances on CBS Radio. Broadcast dates appear in parentheses.)

Lux Radio Theatre: "I Wanted Wings" (March 30, 1942) / With Ray Milland and William Holden.

Stage Door Canteen (October 22, 1942) / With Edmund Gwenn, The Merry Macs, comedian Johnny Burke, and master of ceremonies Bert Lytell.

Lux Radio Theatre: "Sullivan's Travels" (November 9, 1942) / With George Brent and Ralph Bellamy.

Burns 'N' Allen Show (February 16, 1943) / With George Burns, Gracie Allen, Jimmy Cash, and the Paul Whiteman Orchestra.

BLUE RIBBON TOWN (September 11, 1943) / With Groucho Marx, Virginia O'Brien, Donald Dickson, and Kenny Baker.

LUX RADIO THEATRE: "So Proudly We Hail" (November 1, 1943) / *Producer-Director:* Cecil B. DeMille/ With Claudette Colbert, Paulette Goddard, Sonny Tufts, and the Lou Silvers Orchestra.

THE JACK CARSON SHOW (December 8, 1943) / No additional information available.

WHICH IS WHICH? (February 7, 1945) / With Walter Brennan, Basil Rathbone, Barry Fitzgerald, Alan Reed, Richard Himbers and His Orchestra, and master of ceremonies Truman Bradley.

SCREEN GUILD PLAYERS: "This Gun for Hire" (April 2, 1945) / *Producer-Director:* Bill Lawrence/ With Alan Ladd, conductor Wilbur Hatch, and master of ceremonies Truman Bradley.

REQUEST PERFORMANCE (January 20, 1946) / No additional information available.

LUX RADIO THEATRE: "O.S.S." (November 18, 1946) / *Producer-Director:* William Keighley/ With Alan Ladd and conductor Lou Silvers.

THIS IS HOLLYWOOD: "Ramrod" (February 21, 1947) / *Producer:* Frank Woodruff/ With Joel McCrea, conductor Adolph Deutsch, announcer Bernard Dudley, and film columnist Hedda Hopper.

Miss Lake was also featured on one installment of *Exploring the Unknown* for the Mutual Radio Network.

Television

(Network and broadcast dates appear in parentheses. Role follows cast listing.)

LUX VIDEO THEATRE: "Shadow of the Heart" (CBS, October 16, 1950) / Cast not available/ "Young Blind Girl."

THE BERT PARKS SHOW (NBC, November 1, 1950)/ With Betty Ann Grove, Harold Lang, and the Bobby Sherwood Quintet/ Guest.

SATURDAY NIGHT REVUE: "Your Show of Shows" (NBC, November 18, 1950)/ With Sid Caesar, Imogene Coca, Robert Merrill, and Marguerite Piazza/ Guest.

LIGHTS OUT: "Beware This Woman" (NBC, December 4, 1950)/ With Glenn Denning and Paul Andor/ "Mercy Device."

SOMERSET MAUGHAM THEATRE: "The Facts of Life" (NBC, May 14, 1951)/ With Bill Daniels, Jack Lemmon, and Leslie Barry/ "Valerie."

LUX VIDEO THEATRE: "The Blues Street" (CBS, December 17, 1951)/ With Roddy McDowell/ "Nightclub Queen."

CELANESE THEATRE: "Brief Moment" (ABC, February 6, 1952)/ With Burgess Meredith, Robert Sterling, and Tony Ross/ Role not available.

TALES OF TOMORROW: "Flight Overdue" (ABC, March 28, 1952)/ Cast and role unavailable.

PAUL WINCHELL–JERRY MAHONEY SHOW (NBC, October 6, 1952)/ Cast unavailable/ Guest.

TEXACO STAR THEATRE (NBC, October 14, 1952)/ With Milton Berle, Ruth Gilbert, Fred Clark, Arnold Stang, Jimmy Nelson and his dummy Danny O'Day, Charlie Applewhite, and Connie Russell/ Guest.

GOODYEAR PLAYHOUSE: "Better Than Walking" (NBC, October 16, 1952)/ With Darren McGavin, Marcel Hillaire, Dorothy Long, Jack Creley, and Johnny Silver/ "Judy Howard," whose nickname is "Leni."

PAUL WINCHELL–JERRY MAHONEY SHOW (NBC, November 17, 1952)/ Cast unavailable/ Guest.

LUX VIDEO THEATRE: "Thanks for a Lovely Evening" (CBS, January 12, 1953)/ With Jeffrey Lynn and Art Carney/ "Business Executive's Girlfriend."

DANGER: "Inside Straight" (CBS, March 31, 1953)/ Cast unavailable/ "Dice Girl."

BROADWAY TELEVISION THEATRE: "Gramercy Ghost" (Syndicated, January 4, 1954)/ With Richard Hylton/ Role Unavailable.

TONIGHT SHOW (NBC, August 24, 1956)/ With host Steve Allen and jazz cornetist Wild Bill Davidson/ Guest.

YOUR FIRST IMPRESSION (NBC, August 26, 1963)/ With host Dennis James/ Mystery Celebrity.